Tocqueville

Classic Thinkers

Richard T. W. Arthur, *Leibniz*
Terrell Carver, *Marx*
Daniel E. Flage, *Berkeley*
J. M. Fritzman, *Hegel*
Bernard Gert, *Hobbes*
Dale E. Miller, *J. S. Mill*
Joanne Paul, *Thomas More*
A. J. Pyle, *Locke*
James T. Schleifer, *Tocqueville*
Andrew Ward, *Kant*

Tocqueville

James T. Schleifer

polity

First published in 2018 by Polity Press

Polity Press
65 Bridge Street
Cambridge CB2 1UR, UK

Polity Press
101 Station Landing
Suite 300
Medford, MA 02155, USA

ISBN-13: 978-1-5095-1887-6
ISBN-13: 978-1-5095-1888-3(pb)

A catalogue record for this book is available from the British Library.

Library of Congress Cataloging-in-Publication Data

Names: Schleifer, James T., 1942- author.
Title: Tocqueville / James T. Schleifer.
Description: Medford, MA : Polity, 2018. | Series: Classic thinkers | Includes
    bibliographical references and index.
Identifiers: LCCN 2018010024 (print) | LCCN 2018029305 (ebook) | ISBN
    9781509518913 (Epub) | ISBN 9781509518876 (hardback) | ISBN
    9781509518883 (pbk.)
Subjects: LCSH: Tocqueville, Alexis de, 1805-1859–Political and social views. |
    Democracy–Philosophy. | Tocqueville, Alexis de, 1805-1859. De la democratie
    en Amerique. | Tocqueville, Alexis de, 1805-1859. Ancien regime et la
    revolution.
Classification: LCC JC229.T8 (ebook) | LCC JC229.T8 S45 2018 (print) | DDC
    944.0072/02 [B]–dc23
LC record available at https://lccn.loc.gov/2018010024

Typeset in 10.5 on 12 pt Palatino
by Toppan Best-set Premedia Limited
Printed and bound in Great Britain by Clays Ltd, Popson Street, Bungay

For further information on Polity, visit our website: politybooks.com

Contents

Acknowledgments

My special thanks to my wife Alison Pedicord Schleifer, who carefully reviewed successive drafts of this book, both as an initial copyeditor and as a first reader for style, clarity, and substance. Her advice, suggestions, and support along the way have been invaluable. Any remaining errors, shortcomings, or obscurities are my own.

Pittsburgh

For my grandsons, Blaz and Niko

Introduction: Tocqueville's Basic Message and His Intellectual Journey

Alexis de Tocqueville's fame as a political and social theorist rests on two books, *Democracy in America,* published in two parts in 1835 and 1840, and *The Old Regime and the Revolution,* published in 1856 near the end of his life. In those works, his essential message is the providential advance of democracy (or equality) in the modern world and the concurrent demise of the old aristocratic order. Tocqueville attempts to define democracy, sketch its march forward, and reveal the potential consequences, both good and bad, of the ongoing democratic revolution. His constant twin goals are, first, to show his readers how to develop and sustain democratic societies that are stable, free, and prosperous, and, second, to persuade his readers to take responsibility for moving toward that first elusive goal.

Various traits, habitual to Tocqueville, should be kept in mind. He insisted on the interrelatedness of all aspects of society and carefully traced the many ways in which increasing democracy influenced all areas of civil and political society, including how it transformed human attitudes and behavior. He also characteristically avoided final answers and definitive solutions. Instead, he raised enduring questions about the likely impact of democracy on the contemporary world and offered a perceptive catalogue of probable results and possible responses.

Tocqueville does not fit the usual categories as a theorist. He called for "a new political science ... for a world entirely new."[1] And, in his two master works, he presented a number of original ideas and perspectives that we will examine later. He also assumed an arguably exaggerated stance of impartiality, claiming to speak for no particular political party or viewpoint. He even slips away from any of the easy disciplinary labels that we like to use today: he wrote at various times as a foreign observer and travel commentator, an historian, a legal or constitutional specialist, a sociologist, a psychologist or social psychologist, a literary romanticist, a political theorist, a moralist, and a philosopher.

For more than three decades, from the late 1820s to his death in 1859, Tocqueville, as author and politician, posed the same persistent questions about France, in particular, and about modern society, in general. He considered and reconsidered the same social and political themes, pursued the same fundamental purposes, and imagined much the same solutions for the democratic dilemmas he identified. This book assumes the essential unity of his thought from the first volume of *Democracy in America* in 1835, to the second volume in 1840, and then to *The Old Regime* in 1856; it casts these three tomes as almost three parts of the same lifelong work. Numerous parallel passages in his two great books bear witness to this remarkable intellectual consistency.

His ideas were never static, however; to treat them as such would be a considerable error. The story of Tocqueville as a thinker is one of dynamic, ongoing change and development. In the pages that follow, we will examine Tocqueville's mental habits, including his constant reconsideration of ideas, and see him always testing and retesting his views, shifting directions and emphases, and achieving new insights. Unresolved definitions, subtle distinctions, persistent ambiguities, and an impressive intellectual vitality are hallmarks of Tocqueville's thinking and writing. One challenge in our study will be to capture this sense of movement and excitement while presenting the underlying consistency of his bedrock principles and enduring concerns.

Two other serious mistakes would be to rely merely on Tocqueville's principal texts to understand his ideas, or to treat him simply as an author and theorist. *Democracy in America* and *The Old Regime* remain essential for grasping Tocqueville as a thinker. But we will also touch upon many of his other writings, including his essays, articles, speeches, and reports, as well as his study *Of the Penitentiary System in the United States* ... (1833), and his book *Recollections*, published posthumously. We will also make considerable use of Tocqueville's correspondence, his travel diaries to America, England, and Ireland, and the drafts and notes for his major works. All these materials enrich the major texts and frequently clarify Tocqueville's purposes and meanings as a writer and thinker.

This study also assumes the importance of Tocqueville's own experiences (including his journeys to America, England, and Ireland) and especially his role as a political figure. His social and political theories – and particularly what might be called his "political program" – can be better understood against the background of his substantial involvement in the politics of his time. In the pages of *The Old Regime*, Tocqueville famously denounced the philosophers of the eighteenth century who spun out theories without the slightest practical political experience or exposure. He refused to be such a philosopher, detached from the political life of his day. He felt called by family tradition and personal ambition to active public service. He was a man of action as well as a man of thought, a politician as well as a theorist. As we will see, his profile as a political figure during his lifetime was significant. The full portrait of Tocqueville as a thinker requires an appreciation of theory put into action.

This book is intended to be a useful, but concise, introduction to Tocqueville's thought and work, offering a short sketch of his life, examining his major themes and ideas, and discussing his lasting significance and legacy. A word of warning is in order. Given a necessarily limited format, there is danger of oversimplification, of skipping or shortchanging some of the complications, variations, and secondary developments in Tocqueville's thinking and writing. The following effort touches very little, for example, on Tocqueville's own sources. Readers need to remember that the task of portraying Tocqueville as a political and social theorist is far more complex and nuanced than can be accomplished in such a short introductory volume. Nonetheless, by exploring the tensions in his thought between continuity and change, and by revisiting the interplay between theory and action, we will be able to retrace the greater part of a fascinating intellectual journey.

1

Alexis de Tocqueville: A Brief Biography

Time of Preparation (1805–30)

With several good biographical treatments already available, we do not need to recount Alexis de Tocqueville's life in detail here.[1] A brief outline of his biography will serve our purposes. Tocqueville (1805–59) was born into an old aristocratic family, deeply rooted in Normandy, staunchly royalist in politics, and devoutly Catholic in religion. Several members of the family had been imprisoned and guillotined during the French Revolution, and Tocqueville's own mother and father, also thrown into prison, had escaped execution only because of the abrupt end of the Terror in 1794. His mother never completely recovered physically or psychologically from her own imprisonment and the loss of so many close relatives. Constant reminders at home of the violence and excesses of the Revolution and the abiding grief meant that Tocqueville would always be mindful of that period.

His background provided him as well with another more positive heritage. If he was always aware of the grim personal toll of the Revolution, he also cherished the example of the notable historical role played by his maternal great-grandfather, Malesherbes, who had served as an advisor to Louis XVI and had then stepped forward in 1793 to defend his king on trial. This doomed gesture of loyalty led to the arrest of many family members and to Malesherbes's own execution in 1794. During the Restoration of the Bourbon monarchy, from 1814 to 1830, Tocqueville's own father, Hervé de Tocqueville, had a distinguished public career as prefect of various departments in northern France. So Tocqueville's background provided him not only with an initial conservative impulse and a fierce rejection of revolutionary extremism, but also with a deep commitment to public service and a lasting desire to have a significant place in the political world. This dual inheritance would mark Tocqueville's life and work in many ways.

By the late 1820s, a number of Tocqueville's earlier ideas and beliefs had changed considerably. In 1821, while living with his father in Metz, he read Montesquieu, Rousseau, Voltaire, and other Enlightenment authors and experienced what he later called an intellectual earthquake that collapsed his adolescent certainties of faith and left him in a permanent state of doubt. After completing his secondary education, Tocqueville pursued the study of law in Paris, where he became aware of the different social and political theories that were part of the French intellectual ferment of the 1820s, which we will discuss later in this chapter. Tocqueville's legal training influenced his continuing interest in certain topics and, to some degree, his methods of analysis. Tocqueville the lawyer is visible throughout his writings, especially in the notes, drafts, and texts of *Democracy in America* and *The Old Regime*.

In 1827, Tocqueville began his career, becoming *juge auditeur* in Versailles. Although the law was not truly suited to his temperament, his time as a young lawyer resulted in several important friendships, particularly his close bond with his colleague, Gustave de Beaumont. Though very different personalities, Tocqueville and Beaumont had similar intellectual interests and political ambitions. Later, they would travel together to North America, England, and Ireland, share writing projects, and, except for a brief period in the 1840s, remain lifelong friends. As young lawyers, they began a study of political economy by reading Jean-Baptiste Say, and in 1829 and 1830 they attended some of François Guizot's lectures on French civilization at the Sorbonne.

Tocqueville was especially fascinated by the scope of Guizot's approach to the study of history. A passage from his notes on one of Guizot's lectures foreshadows the broad and inclusive treatment of society, politics, and culture that would characterize both *Democracy in America* and *The Old Regime*: "The history of civilization...should...try to embrace everything simultaneously. Man is to be examined in all aspects of his social existence. History must follow the course of his intellectual development in his deeds, his customs, his opinions, his laws, and the monuments of his intelligence.... In a word, it is the whole of man during a given period that must be portrayed."[2]

Significantly, by 1829 Tocqueville already had in mind an underlying reason for examining the development of civilization. He announced the goal to Beaumont: "What we must fashion in ourselves is the political man [*homme politique*]. And to do this, we have to study the history of mankind."[3] The family tradition of public life was not forgotten.

The Making of *Democracy in America* (1830–40)

In July 1830, Tocqueville witnessed yet another revolution in France. The July Revolution put an end to the Bourbon Restoration and ushered in the constitutional July Monarchy, headed by Louis-Philippe, king of the French. Despite his disapproval of the new regime, Tocqueville agreed to swear a required oath of allegiance. But as a member of a family of traditional royalists, he realized that his position was nonetheless compromised. He and Beaumont decided therefore to remove themselves temporarily from the French political scene. The idea of visiting the American republic had attracted Tocqueville for at least a year. So now the two friends conceived the plan of proposing an official eighteen-month mission to the United States to study the American penitentiary system, then at the forefront of prison reform. Hidden behind this project were the desire "to see what a great republic is" and the idea of writing a joint work on America that would draw public attention to the young authors and perhaps lead to more promising future careers.[4]

The French government accepted their proposal, and the two friends left for the New World on April 2, 1831, where they remained for nine months. Although their stay was ultimately shorter than they had planned, they traveled extensively throughout North America. After staying in New York City, they crossed New York State, explored the Great Lakes, visited what was then the frontier in Michigan, spent several days in Montreal and Quebec, journeyed to Boston, then to Philadelphia and Baltimore, headed west to Pittsburgh, went down the Ohio to Cincinnati and Louisville and overland to Memphis, descended the Mississippi to New Orleans, traveled rapidly across the South and back up to Washington, DC, before returning to New York. They sailed for France on February 20, 1832.[5] Their final itinerary was shaped in part by their need to visit certain penitentiaries, by a few impulsive decisions, by accidents and vagaries of weather, and by pressure from the government to abbreviate their mission.

While in North America, Tocqueville and Beaumont established parallel methods of daily work: framing essential questions, talking to Americans, taking on-the-spot notes, filling journals and letters with reflections, reading some essential books, and constantly sharing with each other their discoveries and insights. (Later they would follow the same pattern of conversation, reflection, and writing when traveling together to England and Ireland.) Several months into their journey in America, Tocqueville and Beaumont decided to write separate books, but they continued to collaborate closely as privileged readers and critics of successive drafts of their later works.

After returning to France in March 1832, Tocqueville fell into a nearly unshakeable lethargy, forcing Beaumont from March to November to write almost all their official report on the American prisons. In the end, Tocqueville did some additional research and contributed notes and appendices, but Beaumont was the true author of the study *Of the Penitentiary System in the United States and Its Application in France.* The book appeared in January 1833 and was widely praised, winning the prestigious Montyon Prize from the Académie française. The two young men were beginning to be noticed.

In May 1832, Tocqueville resigned his legal position in support of Beaumont, who had been dismissed from his own post for refusing to get involved in a scandalous case with political overtones. The friends were now doubly free to move ahead with their other American works. From August 3 to September 7, 1833, Tocqueville made his first visit to England, hoping both to see something of American origins and to have a point of comparison to what he had seen in the New World.[6] Not until October did he finally settle in Paris and begin work in earnest on his American book.

Tocqueville wrote quickly, maintaining a rigorous work schedule in pursuit of what he called his "monomania." In addition to his own travel notes and other written materials that he had already carefully indexed by key themes, he relied on an impressive list of official documents and legal and historical studies of "the great republic."[7] His research remains impressive. As he wrote, he asked his father and two brothers, Edouard and Hippolyte, to read his manuscript and to comment in writing. He also discussed his evolving ideas and shared his successive drafts with Beaumont and Louis de Kergorlay, perhaps his closest friend, known since childhood. These two individuals served as his "good instruments of conversation"[8] and the primary judges of his developing book.

Tocqueville returned this service to Beaumont, carefully reading and commenting on the latter's own American work, *Marie, ou l'esclavage aux États-Unis* [*Marie, or Slavery in the United States*], also published in 1835. Beaumont's book, though overshadowed by Tocqueville's *Democracy*, nonetheless enjoyed considerable success, and remains a pioneering exploration of American attitudes toward race.

The first portion of *Democracy in America* was almost immediately hailed as a masterpiece, and the young author as a second Montesquieu. Translations and successive printings and editions quickly followed the initial publication. And in 1838, Tocqueville was invited to become a member of the prestigious Academy of Moral and Political Sciences. After such success, Tocqueville did not immediately return to the planned second portion of his American book. In January 1835 he began to write a *Memoir on Pauperism*,[9] which appeared in April in a local journal in Normandy. (A sequel was partially drafted in 1837, but never published.) This paper, an initial foray into economic issues and matters of social reform, was perhaps designed to prepare the ground for an eventual political effort in the region. The essay was also probably stimulated in part by Tocqueville's meeting, during his brief 1833 visit to England, with the English political economist Nassau William Senior. But perhaps even more significantly, Tocqueville, for this *Memoir*, read a treatise on the problem of poverty, *Economie politique chrétienne* [*Christian Political Economy*] (1834), by Alban de Villeneuve-Bargemont, a French theorist who presented a profound moral critique of unrestrained capitalism. Villeneuve-Bargemont's analysis would especially mark the writing of several chapters of the 1840 *Democracy*. Then, from April to August, Tocqueville, once again in the company of Beaumont, visited England and Ireland. As we will see, this second journey to England influenced Tocqueville's social, political, and economic thinking in several significant ways.

Other events also interrupted work on the 1840 *Democracy*. In October 1835, despite the disapproval of his family and closest friends, Tocqueville married Mary (Marie) Mottley, a middle-class Englishwoman, a union that unintentionally symbolized his later observations that democratic society encouraged interclass marriage. And early in 1836, Tocqueville was busy drafting a paper he had agreed to write for John Stuart Mill on the "Social and Political State of France Before and After 1789." Tocqueville's article, his first published treatment of the old regime and the French Revolution, would appear in the *London and Westminster Review* in April 1836.

Tocqueville and Beaumont spent much of August 1837 together in Normandy working on their upcoming books, including reading and commenting on their respective drafts. In 1839 Beaumont would publish *L'Irelande sociale, politique et religieuse*; and in 1840 Tocqueville would finally present the second part of *Democracy in America*. But that summer their talk and planning also turned to politics. Both Tocqueville and Beaumont always had intense political ambition. Now the two companions each decided to run for election in November 1837 for seats in the Chamber of Deputies. To prepare the ground for a campaign, Tocqueville wrote two significant articles on Algeria.[10] The French conquest and colonization of Algeria, under way since 1830, had prompted a vigorous and ongoing policy debate that he now joined. Tocqueville was gradually marking out three of the major public issues that he would continue to address in his political career: prison reform,[11] the causes of and cures for poverty, and Algeria (and colonization). More such topics of interest would soon emerge. Although the initial campaigns of both Tocqueville and Beaumont were unsuccessful, they did not abandon their political goals.

At the beginning of 1839, Tocqueville put his energies into a second election effort, this time with success. In March he became deputy of Valognes in Normandy, a district he would represent until the end of his political career in 1852. As a new member of the Chamber, he devoted much of the summer of 1839 to a presentation on abolition, his *Report on Slavery in the French Colonies*.[12] The abolition of slavery became yet another of the important public issues that would habitually occupy him in public life.

The second portion of *Democracy in America* finally appeared in 1840. The work received a more mixed reaction than the first volume, striking many readers as being overly philosophical, even speculative. Tocqueville himself recognized the more theoretical nature of the second part of his book, describing it as less about America and more about democracy. Nonetheless, his prestige as a writer and theorist led, in 1841, to membership in the Académie française; at little more than 35 years of age, he had become one of the "forty immortals," as members of the French Academy were called.

In some ways, the 1830s were still a time of preparation for Tocqueville. By the age of 30, he had already written a superb work of social and political theory and brought himself fame and reputation far more permanently than he could have imagined, but much of his activity during the decade, especially his other writings and expanding circle of correspondents and public contacts, may be seen as means to secure a significant political career. The man of letters still longed to become a man of politics.

Homme Politique: Tocqueville the Politician (1839–52)

Tocqueville's role as a political figure tells us something of his efforts to put his theories to work. In *Democracy in America*, as we will observe, Tocqueville proposed a quite specific political program for avoiding democratic dangers and for preserving liberty in the modern democratic age. As a politician, he took positions and pursued policies that help to clarify that program and to define his social and political thinking.

Once elected to the Chamber of Deputies in 1839, Tocqueville began his political career with considerable expectations. For a man not yet 35 years old, he brought an impressive reputation to the Chamber. In August 1840, he shared his hopes with Pierre-Paul Royer-Collard, a prominent political figure during the Restoration, an elder statesman, still a fellow Deputy, and an admirer of Tocqueville and his *Democracy*. As Tocqueville had made clear in the first volume of his book, he longed for a political world based on great principles. Could the petty politics of the July Monarchy be turned in this direction? "Do you believe, Monsieur, that a time may come in which a love of the public good, as disinterested as our poor human nature permits, can render some service and finally put integrity in a place of honor? Will people like me finally have their day?"[13]

Although from the beginning he sat with the center-left opposition, he saw himself as an independent, aligned with no particular party or group. Echoing the call in *Democracy* for honest souls to come together to support a new kind of liberalism, his long-term strategy was to develop and lead a new coalition of the moderate like-minded. Nothing of this plan came to pass. The Chamber prized eloquent discourse from the tribune, and Tocqueville's public speaking skills were hampered by his voice, natural reticence, and tendency to burden his speeches with too much subtlety, as though he were writing. He also seemed unable to treat most of his colleagues with genuine warmth and friendliness; his ability to relate on a personal level to those not part of his own class remained painfully limited. Was it snobbery, or shyness, or simply an inborn coldness? In any case, he always felt something of an outsider, standing apart from his fellows. He soon found himself quite isolated in the Chamber – respected, but unable to rally any band of close supporters to his own views and principles.

By the end of 1841, Tocqueville, in another letter to Royer-Collard, expressed his frustration with "our miserable political world." He admitted that he detested the two most prominent political leaders at the time in the Chamber, Louis-Adolphe Thiers and François Guizot. Complaining about his isolation and powerlessness, he wrote: "I compare myself to a wheel that goes around very quickly, but which, having missed its gear, does nothing and is useful for nothing."[14] But, as we will see, he exaggerated his own uselessness.

As a member of the Chamber of Deputies from 1839 to 1848, Tocqueville's primary engagements, in speeches, committee work, reports, and articles, involved the public issues already noted – prison reform, the causes of and cures for poverty and related social questions, Algeria and colonization, and the abolition of slavery – as well as others he would address – foreign policy and the stature of France in the world, electoral reform, and education. After 1848, he would also become closely identified with constitutional reform.

Tocqueville began in 1842 to align himself more closely with the circle around Odilon Barrot, an important political figure and opposition leader in the Chamber of Deputies. He worried increasingly in the 1840s about the broadening appeal of socialism, the increasing attacks on the principle of private property, and the growing risk of yet another revolution. Social reform proposals were his first response to this concern about rising radicalism. As he explained to Lord Radnor: "There is only one way to avert and attenuate the revolution, which is to do everything that is possible to ameliorate the lot of the people before being forced to do so."[15] He began to set forth a specific program of reforms echoing some of the social and political ideas in *Democracy in America*. In January 1843, he wrote six letters in the newspaper *Le Siècle* on the political situation in France, denouncing excessive materialism, warning against growing social and economic inequalities, and suggesting some possible solutions.[16] An editorial statement and a series of articles in 1844 and 1845 in *Le Commerce*, a journal owned for a short time by Tocqueville and a small group of friends, again advocated a number of specific social and economic changes.[17] And in 1847, as part of a Manifesto, ultimately never published, Tocqueville detailed several measures to help the poor and working classes.[18] We will examine some of these reform proposals more closely later.

Sensing the growing danger of social and political upheaval, his second impulse was to awaken his colleagues. In January 1848, before the Chamber, he issued a blunt prediction of the coming upheaval.

Within a month, the Revolution he feared broke out. A cascade of events followed:

- the end of the July Monarchy and the announcement (unofficial) of the Second Republic (February 1848);
- the convening of the Constituent Assembly (May 1848);
- the June Days, a more radical and violent popular uprising, put down with ferocity by the forces of order (June 1848);
- the drafting, discussion, and approval of a new constitution (May to November 1848);
- the election, for a four-year term, of Louis-Napoleon Bonaparte as President of the Republic (December 1848);
- the first meeting of the Legislative Assembly (May 1849);
- the efforts, unsuccessful, to amend the constitution to allow Louis-Napoleon to have a second consecutive term as president (May to August 1851);
- the *coup d'état* by Louis-Napoleon (December 1851); and
- the proclamation of the Second Empire (December 1852).

Tocqueville took part in these events in multiple and important ways. His various roles as a political figure between 1848 and 1852 can also be briefly catalogued. He was elected to the Constituent Assembly in April 1848, from his home district, by what was then called "universal" (adult male) suffrage. In May 1848, he was chosen, on the first ballot, by his colleagues in the Assembly to serve on the Constitutional Committee, charged with drafting a constitution for the Second Republic. In May the following year, he was elected, under the new constitution, to the Legislative Assembly (where he sat with the center-right). A month later, Odilon Barrot named him Minister of Foreign Affairs, a post he held only until October when the Barrot government fell. From May to August 1851, he was prominently involved in efforts to amend the constitution, and in December, he was arrested and imprisoned for three days during the *coup d'état*. The following year, he refused to take an oath of allegiance to Louis-Napoleon's government and withdrew from public life, resigning even from his local offices.

Conventional wisdom – and even some of what we earlier recounted about Tocqueville's political career – stresses his failure to achieve his own goals and his own sense of frustration at how little he was able to accomplish. But his political trajectory can be seen quite differently. Between 1839 and 1852, he was re-elected to local, as well as national, office by increasing margins, under both very restricted and universal suffrage, during both the July regime and the Second Republic. He was selected by his peers to be a member of the Constitutional Committee, as well as the special commission charged with revising the constitution. Widely respected and recognized as ministerial caliber, he served briefly as Minister of Foreign Affairs and was considered for other cabinet positions. All this activity came to an end with the *coup d'état* in 1851, but although Louis-Napoleon sought to assuage Tocqueville and to elicit his support, he was unsuccessful.

Perhaps, as André Jardin once suggested, Tocqueville's greatest political failure was his early death. Given his unyielding rejection of Louis-Napoleon's actions and regime, his reputation for personal integrity, and his lifelong commitment to free democratic institutions, Tocqueville may yet have served France in high positions, after the end of the Second Empire, during the early years of the Third Republic in the 1870s. A dramatically successful entry might possibly have been added to his political portfolio. Jardin's comment remains speculative, but it is at least worth considering.

To come to terms with the Revolution of 1848, especially the violence of the June Days, Tocqueville decided to write candidly about the events and the major players, but to do so privately. His account, composed during 1850 and 1851, was meant for posthumous publication only. Such was the formula for his *Recollections*, a work unlike Tocqueville's other major writings, both because of the intense emotions and unrestrained opinions expressed and because the work, not intended for a wide audience, remained unpublished until 1893, long after Tocqueville's death.

The Making of *The Old Regime and the Revolution* (1850–59)

Tocqueville's definitive withdrawal from political life in 1852 did not mean the end of his efforts to address the public. His voice shifted from political discourse and action back to the written page. In the 1840s, on two occasions, Tocqueville had presented formal remarks on the French Revolution and Napoleon, returning to themes first touched upon in his 1836 essay on the social and political state of France before and after 1789.[19] The subject of the causes and consequences of the great Revolution never ceased to attract him.

As early as 1850, even before Louis-Napoleon's seizure of power, Tocqueville had begun planning another book, initially conceived as a history of the first Napoleon and his Empire. In 1852 and 1853 he pushed ahead, undertaking intensive research, significantly shifting his focus, and composing what would become *The Old Regime and the Revolution,* published in 1856. The work presented a strikingly original historical analysis. Centralization, Tocqueville argued, did not arise out of the Revolution and its aftermath, but instead long predated the collapse of the old regime. By undermining effective political participation and destroying civic engagement, centralization was in fact a basic cause rather than a result of the Revolution. The book, with its novel message, was well received, and Tocqueville began to write a second volume, focused on the Revolution itself and the coming of the Empire. This work would unfortunately remain incomplete, existing only as partial drafts and extensive notes.

As a writer, Tocqueville did not give up either his impulse for serious research or his use of Beaumont and Kergorlay as favorite judges of his ideas and emerging text. While drafting *The Old Regime,* he thoroughly immersed himself in archival materials, in Paris, London, Germany, and especially Tours, where he lived for a year. Indeed, his impressive research methods remain a hallmark of this second great book. But if such painstaking mining of archives was unusual at the time, the careful effort to identify, gather, and use essential sources repeated Tocqueville's approach as he wrote *Democracy.* And once again, with *The Old Regime,* Beaumont and Kergorlay served as readers and critics of the manuscript. Successive drafts passed repeatedly by their eyes and ears.

The Old Regime also testifies to Tocqueville's habit of constantly reconsidering his fundamental ideas, giving them new twists, or even pushing them in unexpected directions. In his 1856 volume, for example, he focused less on democracy and more on liberty and revolution. He shifted from his earlier concept of *individualism* to the notion of what he called *collective individualism,* the tendency of each class or group within a society toward isolation, self-absorption, mutual hostility, and non-involvement in any public life. He explored more fully the influence of ideas on society. And he gave greater attention to analyzing the nature of aristocracy, especially the distinction between a healthy and a useless (even parasitic) aristocratic class.

Despite these and other differences, both obvious and not so obvious, *The Old Regime* and *Democracy in America* also share many similarities, particularly in such themes as the political, social, and moral dangers of centralization, the importance of public participation and practical political experience, the crucial role of mores, and the inescapable link between the social and political dimensions of society. Tocqueville himself stressed the connections between the two works, especially his central purpose: showing readers how to create and maintain a free democratic society. "The unity of my life and thought," he declared in 1856 to his friend Jean-Jacques Ampère, "is the most important thing which I need to maintain before the public eye; the man is as involved in that as the writer."[20]

Tocqueville had never been robust. But in 1850, in the midst of the tumultuous events described above, he had his first serious attack of the tuberculosis that would prove fatal within a few years. Forced to take a six-month leave from the legislature, he turned his absence to good account by beginning work on his *Recollections*. Throughout the 1850s his health continued to deteriorate, and he was often ill. Advancing sickness only added to his discouragement about the political future of France, but Tocqueville found a sense of purpose in writing *The Old Regime*; after withdrawing from public life, he devoted his declining energies to work on that book.

In the summer of 1858, Tocqueville's physical state worsened alarmingly. Advised to spend the winter in southern France, he and his wife, who was also seriously ill, went to Cannes. Members of Tocqueville's family and a few of his closest friends, including Beaumont and Kergorlay, began to gather, some staying for weeks to provide company and support. On March 4, 1859, at a moment when members of his faithful band had temporarily dispersed, Tocqueville wrote an urgent letter to Beaumont. "My dear friend, I know nothing that has ever grieved me so much as what I am going to say to you: *I ask you to come*. Here we are all alone.... If ever you could do something good for us, it is now.... What can I say to you, my friend, if not this: COME. COME, as fast as you can. *You alone* can put us back on the field."[21] Beaumont arrived, staying about three weeks, but Tocqueville never regained his health, dying on April 16, 1859. He was only 53 years old.

Some Biographical Remarks

Having rapidly reviewed Tocqueville's biography we need to underscore several constant themes of his life. As already noted, Tocqueville was a man of great ambition, hungering for recognition and esteem and driven to assume a prominent role in public life. "My nature," he wrote to Royer-Collard in 1841, "is to be active and, I must admit, ambitious."[22] If he genuinely loved the world of ideas, one of his purposes as an author was also to open the door to effective political action.

Two common assumptions about Tocqueville need to be amended. The first we have already addressed, noting that his political career was far from a story of failure. The second involves his reputation as someone rather cold, even off-putting. For later biographers, he provided a devastating self-portrait in his *Recollections* of a man unable to remember the names of ordinary or undistinguished colleagues.[23] But throughout his life he had a core of close friends, among them Louis de Kergorlay, Gustave de Beaumont, the brothers Eugène and Charles Stoffels, and Jean-Jacques Ampère. He should perhaps be regarded less as a creature of habitual aloofness and more as a man of warm and intimate friendships.

Tocqueville knew himself well. He recognized his own persistent restlessness, anxiety, and discontent, characteristics that he would identify more generally in his *Democracy* and elsewhere as chronic to democratic times. In 1840, he described to his brother Edouard "this anxiety of mind, this devouring impatience ... this disposition [that] gives me a great élan in certain moments. But most often it torments without cause, agitates fruitlessly ... I am often unhappy without reason."[24]

In a letter to Madame Sophie Swetchine, written in 1856 near the end of his life, he also admitted to a "sort of sickly sadness by which I have been tormented from time to time throughout my life."[25] André Jardin and other biographers have mentioned this depressive tendency. Perhaps this recurring melancholy simply reflected the expected emotions of his Romantic age. But Tocqueville's periodic feelings of despondency and dejection appear to be more than simply fashionable sentiments; his chronic bouts of depression echo his mother's illnesses and seem to reveal something of his essential personality.

We also need to acknowledge Tocqueville's rejection of absolutes and preference for probabilities. As we have observed, at the age of 16, after reading various Enlightenment authors discovered in his father's library, Tocqueville famously underwent a profound spiritual and intellectual revolution. A few years later, he described this painful experience to his friend Charles Stoffels: "When I first began to reflect, I believed that the world was full of demonstrated truths. ... But when I sought to apply myself to considering the objects, I perceived nothing but inevitable doubts. ... I ultimately convinced myself that the search for absolute, demonstrable truth ... was an effort directed toward the impossible. It is not that there are not some truths that merit man's complete conviction, but be sure they are very few in number. Concerning the immense majority of points that it is important for us to know, we have only probabilities, almosts."[26]

Each of these character traits helped to shape Tocqueville's writings and actions in a variety of ways. His lifelong tendency toward pessimism only grew more marked by the 1850s and increasingly colored his writings. Perceptive readers have often noted the growing darkness in his three books written in 1835, 1840, and 1856. In the 1850s, after the rise of Louis-Napoleon, he was at times deeply discouraged, even angry and bitter.[27] But we need to recognize, as well, that Tocqueville never fully lost hope in the possibility of free and healthy democratic societies. He was always able to step back from the brink of despair. As he had declared to Kergorlay in 1835, "I cannot believe that for several centuries God has pushed two or three million men toward equality of conditions in order to bring them in the end to ... despotism."[28]

The conviction that liberty could survive in democratic times would never entirely leave him. As late as 1857, two years before his death, Tocqueville reprimanded Arthur de Gobineau for his grim pessimism, reminding his friend that the enterprise of maintaining liberty in democratic societies, though difficult, was not impossible. "No, I will not believe that this human species ... should become [a] debased flock ... and that there is nothing more to do than to deliver it ... to a small number of shepherds ... You will permit me to have less confidence in you than in the [goodness] and justice of God."[29]

His rejection of absolutes, his insistence on *probabilities* and *almosts*, especially colored his message as a social and political theorist. This personal perspective pushed him, for example, to accept an idea he had first found in Montesquieu. As he drafted the first volume of *Democracy*, he mused: "Ideas for the preface ... I do not even believe that there is anything in institutions of an absolute good. Montesquieu."[30] Writing to his father from America, he asserted even more bluntly: "The more I see of this country, the more convinced I am of the following truth: that there is virtually no political institution that is radically good or radically bad in itself, and everything depends on the physical conditions and the social state of the people to which it is applied."[31]

Finally, we need to note several other constants in the thread of Tocqueville's life. He never lost touch with America. He continued to correspond with American friends and kept himself informed about events there. With growing alarm, he followed, for example, the worsening tensions between North and South during the 1850s and recognized the increasing likelihood of civil war.[32] Nor did he forget England and his English correspondents. In the summer of 1857, he even made a third visit to England.

Tocqueville's thinking was constantly evolving. During the 1840s and 1850s, it continued to develop, just as it had during the 1820s and during the making of his *Democracy* in the 1830s. But, in part, Tocqueville's life after 1840 can be seen as his effort to apply some of the ideas and principles expressed in *Democracy in America*. His activities served, first, as his own exercise in political participation, as his own commitment to civic life. Second, his career provided opportunities to test his ideas, to put them to work, to link theory and practice. And once the door of politics was closed, Tocqueville, as author of *The Old Regime*, turned to the project of working out the application of his ideas to another time and nation.

Tocqueville's life, in sum, oscillated between two roles: author of books and political actor. Both the life of the mind and the life of public service attracted him and fired his considerable ambition. We need always to remember that Tocqueville the social and political theorist was at once a literary and a political figure.[33]

Tocqueville's Intellectual Context

Before moving ahead, we need briefly to present a few of Tocqueville's major sources and examine his intellectual context. Such a presentation is an essential part of any biographical sketch of Tocqueville as a theorist. His sources were many and remarkably diverse. As available bibliographies demonstrate, the breadth of works he consulted for writing both *Democracy in America* and *The Old Regime* remains impressive.[34] But in addition to readings – of all types, on a variety of topics, and across many time frames – his sources include travel and first-hand observation in North America, England, Ireland, and Germany; interviews and conversations, some of which continued intermittently over decades; archival research; correspondence that often became dialogues by pen maintained for years; and of course political experiences on the local, regional, and national levels from the late 1830s to the 1850s. Tocqueville's intellectual starting points, broadly understood, embrace both the traditional and predictable, as well as more informal and innovative elements.

Tocqueville habitually and famously did not fully disclose many of his sources. References found in the drafts and manuscripts for both his major works disclose more extensive use of certain writings and authors than are indicated in his texts; and sometimes his papers reveal new, completely unacknowledged points of reference. So it remains difficult to identify Tocqueville's sources in any definitive way. Moreover, his many sources not only served him as points of origin or inspiration for certain ideas or themes, but also functioned, at times, as foils, as stimulants for the consideration and development of contrary viewpoints. Careful readers have found, for example, hidden in the pages of the *Democracy* or *The Old Regime*, extensive virtual dialogues between Tocqueville and Montesquieu, or Edmund Burke, or François Guizot.[35]

If we focus on intellectual antecedents, we can confirm Tocqueville's familiarity with authors of the classical world, especially Plato, whom he praised for aspiring "toward immortality and the infinite" and for addressing "great principles of the beautiful and the good."[36] Tocqueville also knew various writers of the Renaissance, particularly Machiavelli, whom he recognized as astute, but criticized as fundamentally amoral. He read these two figures, as well as others, not rapidly or superficially, but "with reflection and deliberateness."[37] Their ideas became part of his general mental background.

Among the more significant influences on Tocqueville, however, were French authors of the seventeenth century, including Jacques-Bénigne Bossuet, Bishop of Meaux, and especially Pascal. In Bossuet, famous for his eloquent sermons and books on religious history, Tocqueville encountered the powerful idea that history unfolded according to providential design. Pascal's works seemed to hold a special attraction for Tocqueville, who remarked that he read a bit of Pascal, as well as Montesquieu and Rousseau, almost daily. In his own writings, he clearly reflected Pascal's sense of serious moral expectation and concern for the human soul and spirit. To a considerable degree, Tocqueville's most basic assumptions about the purpose of life and about human responsibility mirrored what he had learned from Pascal.

Two of the great figures of the eighteenth-century French Enlightenment, Montesquieu and Rousseau, also profoundly shaped Tocqueville's thinking and writing. (In later chapters we will recount Tocqueville's engagement with some other eighteenth-century writers.) Montesquieu's style helped to stimulate Tocqueville's own clear and elegant prose. And some of Montesquieu's basic themes – such as insistence on the value of intermediary bodies; praise for the separation and balance of powers, including an independent judiciary; and recognition of the connections between liberty and commerce – reappeared in Tocqueville's works. Tocqueville especially admired his predecessor's approach and tone as a theorist. He echoes Montesquieu's preference for moderation, his comparative method, his habit of examining topics from a variety of viewpoints, his liking for broad analysis or what might be called philosophical history, and his emphasis on *spirit* or *general spirit* as the defining feature of a nation, a concept similar to Tocqueville's notion of *mores*, which we will discuss later. Unlike Montesquieu, however, Tocqueville looked not to England, but to the American republic as a point of comparison.[38]

Rousseau's influence is less obvious and more difficult to define. Tocqueville repeats Rousseau's perspective on the origin of inequality in human society. And he seems to share his predecessor's general view of human nature or human psychology. However, Tocqueville, by implication at least, denounced Rousseau's concept of popular sovereignty and of the omnipotence of the general will. In the 1835 volume of *Democracy in America*, he declared: "I regard as impious and detestable this maxim that in matters of government the majority of a people has the right to do anything."[39] Tocqueville, like some other writers among his contemporaries, blamed Rousseau, in part, for the excesses and violence of the French Revolution.

As already mentioned, France during the early nineteenth century and particularly in the 1820s was a place of remarkable creativity in social and political ideas.[40] A number of significant writers at that time searched for the possible foundations of a stable, free, and prosperous society in the face of a divisive revolutionary past and an emerging new social, political, and economic world. These theorists numbered some in the classic liberal tradition, such as Benjamin Constant, and included others, known as *doctrinaires*, especially Pierre-Paul Royer-Collard, François Guizot, and Charles de Rémusat. Together, these writers shaped Tocqueville's intellectual context even more directly than earlier authors that he read.

Constant shared Tocqueville's critique of Rousseau's idea of popular sovereignty, arguing that the will of the people was not unlimited; for Constant, as well as for Tocqueville, absolute power of any type and in any hands was unacceptable. Tocqueville also appreciated Constant's stress on liberty as individual rights; but, as we will discover, he broadened the concept of liberty by insisting not only on the independent individual, but also on civic engagement and the practice of liberty in order to secure true freedom. Finally, both writers worried about the decline of public life as private matters became increasingly important in the modern age.

The political reformers called the *doctrinaires* addressed many of the themes that became central to Tocqueville's own thought, such as the coming of democracy, an understanding of democracy as both social and political, the rise of the middle class, the dangers of concentrated or unchecked power, the pursuit of the best protections for liberty – including basic rights, local liberties, associations, and freedom of the press – the search for the middle way, and, perhaps most fundamentally, the effort to end revolution and achieve social and political stability.[41] The topics that drew their attention provide a kind of checklist for Tocqueville's own concerns.

Royer-Collard, important theorist and political leader during the Bourbon Restoration, remained active in the 1830s, and served as something of a mentor to Tocqueville. Their relationship rested on great mutual admiration. Royer-Collard advocated local liberties and associations, in particular, as buffers against centralized power and upheld freedom of the press as an essential liberty.

Guizot probably ranked as the most important of the *doctrinaires*. As an historian and lecturer, his broad view of history, his sense of how all aspects of a society are interconnected, and his vision of advancing civilization all captured Tocqueville's close attention in the late 1820s, as already noted. Guizot also became one of the political leaders of the July Monarchy and served, for a brief time, as Prime Minister. As a politician, he drew the condemnation of Tocqueville, who accused him of abandoning his principles.[42] As a theorist, Guizot endorsed the division of powers, bicameralism, freedom of the press, and trial by jury, all of which resonated with Tocqueville. The two writers differed, however, on their attitudes toward the middle class and toward political democracy. For Guizot, the ascendance of the middle class marked the culmination of historical development; Tocqueville, in contrast, doubted that the middle class was able to govern and see beyond its own narrow interests. And for Guizot, *political* democracy needed to be hedged in by limited suffrage; only those who had demonstrated the moral and material capacity to govern (essentially the social and economic elite) deserved a political voice and a part in representative government. Tocqueville, as we will observe, believed that, to achieve stability in the modern world, social democracy had to be matched with political democracy. Guizot also saw England as a model; whereas Tocqueville, at least in *Democracy*, looked primarily to America.

More broadly, Tocqueville was less pessimistic about the democratic future than the *doctrinaires*, especially Guizot. He argued that the best could be made of democracy, that the way to moderate democracy was to offer more democracy, and that political democracy could be made less dangerous by promoting, instead of suppressing, public participation. Tocqueville, as we will see, also developed, in the 1840 volume of *Democracy*, a powerful vision of a new sort of democratic despotism, quite unimagined by the *doctrinaires*, who worried about more traditional forms of democratic excess.

Nonetheless, the imprint of the *doctrinaires* on Tocqueville's social and political theory is evident. To a degree, the creative ideas that emerged in France during the 1820s provided a basic intellectual framework for the author of *Democracy in America* and *The Old Regime*. But his views were not set by 1830. As we move ahead, we will see Tocqueville – in response to travels, first-hand observations, exchanges by letter and in person, further readings, political experiences, and direct witness of successive changes of regimes and outbreaks of revolutionary violence and the coming of a new despot – considering, reconsidering, and revising his ideas.

The undeniable influence of his intellectual contemporaries raises yet other issues. What makes Tocqueville original? Why do we study him so widely, but mostly ignore the writings of Guizot and the other *doctrinaires*? What continues to draw readers to Tocqueville? In later chapters, we will return to these questions and try to bring out his originality and his continuing appeal as a social and political theorist.

2

First Principles

Democracy on the March

Later chapters in this book will explore the development and complexities of Tocqueville's major themes in social and political theory. Here our goal is to present some of the most important underlying and (mostly) unchanging concepts in his writings, to consider what might be called Tocqueville's first principles. This effort will also reveal a few of his favorite terms and habits of thinking and writing.

Tocqueville announced his most basic conviction, the ongoing democratic revolution, in both his major works. From his Introduction to the first volume of *Democracy in America* to the text of *The Old Regime*, he presented the same fundamental message. "[As] I studied American society," he wrote in 1835, "I saw more and more, in equality of conditions, the generating fact from which each particular fact seemed to derive, and I rediscovered it constantly before me as a central point where all of my observations came together. Then I turned my thought back toward our hemisphere ... and this same democracy that reigned in American societies, appeared to me to advance rapidly toward power in Europe. ... A great democratic revolution is taking place among us."[1]

He then sketched a brilliant summary of 700 years of French history, linking all major events and developments to the march of democracy.[2] As a theorist, Tocqueville sometimes used the concept of a main or mother idea (*idée mère*) that served as a central starting point and generated a host of subsequent ideas and consequences. Arguably, his thesis of an ongoing democratic revolution was the mother idea for the entire body of his work.

In 1848, in the Foreword to the twelfth edition of *Democracy in America*, he reaffirmed this basic principle by reproducing his own words from 1835: "The gradual development of equality of conditions is a providential fact; ... it is universal, it is lasting, it escapes every day from human power; all events, like all men, serve its development."[3] And in a note to *The Old Regime* in 1856, as he reflected on the reasons for the decline of feudal institutions, he again asserted: "[The] general cause was the passage from one social state to another, from feudal inequality to democratic equality."[4]

Tocqueville's consistency over three decades is noteworthy, but his declarations also illustrate the way in which he shifted, perhaps too easily, from equality of conditions, to democracy, to democratic revolution, to democratic equality, using the words almost interchangeably. And what did he mean by *social state*, a concept essential to his definitions of democracy, his understanding of democratic and aristocratic societies, and his explanation of equality of conditions?

Tocqueville dedicated the third chapter of the 1835 volume of *Democracy* to the "Social State of the Anglo-Americans," and there described the origins, development, and varieties of equality in colonial America. He began his discussion with an attempt at definition. "I will speak so frequently about the social state of the Anglo-Americans that, first and foremost, I need to say what I mean by the words *social state*. In my view, the social state is the material and intellectual condition in which a people finds itself in a given period. The social state is ordinarily the result of a fact, sometimes of laws, more often of these two causes together. But once it exists, it can itself be considered the first cause of most of the laws, customs and ideas that regulate the conduct of nations; what it does not produce, it modifies."[5]

Apparently even Tocqueville found this effort vague and unsatisfying.[6] The meaning of the term remained elusive. How did social state relate to equality of conditions or to democracy? How was the "first cause" itself produced and shaped? In Tocqueville's social and political theory, this would not be the only significant concept with a plastic and ultimately indeterminate meaning. The chronic tendency to slip over firm definitions remains one of Tocqueville's inescapable mental characteristics.

Three Causes: Circumstances, Laws, and Mores

Tocqueville was never single-minded. As an historian and theorist, he recognized a host of causes when he told the story of any nation or society. Some, which he usually labeled accidental or particular, were ranked as secondary causes. These included, for example, the size of capital cities, the level of commercial activity or financial complexity, and the absence of dangerous military heroes, as well as the element of chance. In his *Recollections*, he summarized his viewpoint. "I believe that many important historical facts can be explained only by accidental circumstances, while many others are inexplicable, and finally, that chance – or, rather, that skein of secondary causes that we call chance because we cannot untangle them – plays a major part in everything that takes place on the world stage. But I also firmly believe that chance accomplishes nothing for which the groundwork has not been laid in advance."[7]

For Tocqueville, however, discovering how to explain the history, the success, or failure of any given society involved more than identifying a multitude of miscellaneous causes. As he traveled in the United States in 1831, he kept this puzzle of causation in mind and several times in his travel notes drew up preliminary lists of likely reasons why the American republic seemed to prosper and flourish.[8] By 1834, as he drafted the first volume of *Democracy in America*, Tocqueville settled on his ultimate explanation, naming circumstances, laws, and mores (*moeurs*) as the three fundamental causes for the historical path of a nation or people. Of this trinity, the most important was mores.

Circumstances, for Tocqueville, included both physical or geographic characteristics and historical beginnings and developments (origins). His definition of circumstances remained fluid, however. As he wrote *Democracy in America*, physical or material circumstances, including climate, geographic position, and resources, faded somewhat in favor of historical circumstances, antecedent facts, or *point of departure*, another of Tocqueville's favorite terms.[9]

In 1835, after describing the physical circumstances of North America in the opening chapter of *Democracy in America*, he turned his attention to history in the second chapter, "Of the Point of Departure and Its Importance for the Future of the Anglo-Americans," where he retraced the colonial laws and mores of the first inhabitants of New England.[10] The search for origins even drove Tocqueville in 1833, as we have noted, to travel to England for the first time to explore the American starting point. This growing stress on point of departure would become even more striking in the 1850s as Tocqueville planned *The Old Regime*. His initial interest was to write about Napoleon and his Empire, but he soon realized that such a project required treatment of the causes and course of the Revolution itself. Tocqueville found himself looking at the old regime in order to uncover the roots of the events of 1789 and after. *The Old Regime and the Revolution* was itself testimony to the importance for Tocqueville of the point of departure and historical circumstances.

Laws in Tocqueville's thinking embraced legal and political institutions, as well as constitutional structures. The term signaled both the work of ordinary legislators and that of the makers of fundamental laws; it also called to mind the rights and duties of citizens, the organizations and activities of civil society, and the powers and functions of the various branches of government. For Tocqueville, laws meant the particular institutional and structural thicket that defined the unique contours of every society.

Mores involved an even broader cluster. "I apply [the expression mores] not only to mores strictly speaking, which could be called *habits of the heart*, but to the different notions that men possess, to the diverse opinions that are current among them, and to the ensemble of ideas from which the *habits of the mind* are formed. So by this word I understand the whole moral and intellectual state of a people."[11]

Among the diverse elements of mores, ideas held a privileged and increasingly important place in Tocqueville's analysis. Ideas could drive history. In 1835 he stressed the seminal influence of Puritanism on the future of the American republic. In his *Recollections* and related speeches and letters, socialist theories played a similar key role in producing the events of 1848, especially the terrible June Days of violent class warfare. And in *The Old Regime*, the social and political schemes of the *philosophes*, the men of letters of the eighteenth century, worked powerfully to cause and to shape the nature of the French Revolution. For Tocqueville, it can be argued, habits of the mind – opinions, beliefs, notions, theories, ideas – were as significant as habits of the heart, an understanding of mores sometimes overlooked by his readers.

In the 1835 *Democracy*, Tocqueville insisted "that maintaining democratic institutions in the United States had to be attributed to circumstances, laws and mores." But he argued further that circumstances counted less than laws, and laws less than mores. "These three great causes undoubtedly serve to regulate and direct American democracy; but if they had to be classified, I would say that physical causes contribute less than laws, and laws infinitely less than mores.... The importance of mores is a common truth to which study and experience constantly lead. It seems to me that I find it placed in my mind like a central point; I see it at the end of all my ideas."[12]

In 1853, nearly twenty years after the publication of the first volume of *Democracy* and while he was drafting *The Old Regime*, Tocqueville wrote to his friend Francisque de Corcelle: "You know my ideas well enough to know that I accord institutions only a secondary influence on the destiny of men. ... I am quite convinced that political societies are not what their laws make them, but what sentiments, beliefs, ideas, habits of the heart, and the spirit of ... men ... prepare them to be."[13] He warned in the pages of the planned second volume of *The Old Regime*: "[One] must not attribute too much power to these particular procedures of the lawmaker. It is men's ideas and passions, not the mechanics of the law, which determine human affairs."[14] (Passions as an element of mores would become increasingly important in Tocqueville's thinking after the February Revolution of 1848.)

For him, the principle of three causes and the primacy of mores applied not only to the American republic, but also to France and other nations.[15] He never deviated from his belief that mores, rather than economic systems, political structures, or physical and material characteristics, held the privileged place for understanding and explaining the trajectory of nations. This viewpoint, echoing Montesquieu, remains one of the hallmarks of Tocqueville's social and political theory.

If Tocqueville's decision to list mores as first among the three general causes remained unwavering, his ranking of circumstances and laws among major causes did shift as he drafted the 1835 *Democracy*. Perhaps the narrowing definition of circumstances helped, but the major reason for this change is telling. At one point, he put the influence of circumstances above that of laws. "Of the three causes the least influential is that of laws and it is, so to speak, the only one which depends on man. ... People cannot change their position and the original conditions of their existence. A nation can, in the long run, modify its habits and its mores, but one generation cannot succeed in doing it. It [a single generation] can only change the laws. ... Not only does man exercise no power over his surroundings, but he possesses, so to speak, none over himself and remains almost completely a stranger to his own fate." When he realized the moral implications of this viewpoint, however, he changed his mind and, revising his draft, reached the conclusion that he would present in 1835 and uphold in all his subsequent works. "So of the three causes which work together to maintain institutions the least essential is the only one that man cannot create at will [circumstances], and God, by making their happiness depend particularly on laws and mores, has in a way placed it in their hands. So physical causes contribute less to the maintenance of institutions than laws; laws, less than mores."[16]

According to Tocqueville, the working of laws put human destiny at least partly in human hands. Although mores change very slowly, they are not immutable; laws can, over time, shape mores. For Tocqueville the moralist, the power of laws left room for human freedom and responsibility. For Tocqueville the patriot, the ability of laws to improve mores offered hope that France could overcome some of the corrosive habits of heart and mind among his countrymen that he so lamented.

The Complexity of Society

Tocqueville preferred a broad, inclusive approach to the history of nations. This chosen perspective – echoing what he had learned from Guizot – arose from yet another first principle. He was convinced that all facets of society, including social, political, religious, economic, intellectual, cultural, behavioral, and others, are intimately interconnected in complex ways. This assumption led Tocqueville to reject simple, uniform explanations of historical, social, or political developments.

In *The Old Regime*, he argued that the *philosophes* had expressed contempt for "complicated and traditional customs," had proposed "general and abstract theories of government," and had "slowly built an imaginary society in which everything seemed simple and coordinated, uniform, equitable, and in accord with reason."[17] He denounced this "unitary spirit," "the idea of ... a general and uniform legislation, everywhere the same, the same for all,"[18] which flowed, Tocqueville wrote bitterly, from a complete lack of practical political experience and an appalling ignorance of how society worked in reality.

Tocqueville's broad vision of the workings of society also led him to see and affirm that forces other than the advance of democracy influenced the path of modern nations. He was not exclusive as a theorist. In discarded drafts of the second volume of *Democracy in America*, for example, he observed, predictably, "Equality is the great fact of our time," but then added, more surprisingly, "Industrial development [is] the second. Both augment the power of government or rather the two are only one."[19]

"I must immediately warn the reader," he wrote in his Foreword to the 1840 *Democracy*, "against an error that would be very prejudicial to me. Seeing me attribute so many diverse effects to equality, he could conclude that I consider equality as the unique cause of all that happens today. This would assume a very narrow view on my part.... Different causes,... distinct from the fact of equality, [are] found in Europe and...explain a great part of what is happening there. I recognize the existence of all these different causes and their power, but talking about them is not my subject."[20] Tocqueville's social and political analysis allowed for more complexities than he could address. As an author, he had to make choices. As readers, we need to appreciate Tocqueville's own admission of a partial and incomplete view.

With the perspective of complex linkage in mind, he also argued that a perceptive observer could discover in a small detail of behavior the broad nature of a given society. "There are a thousand means indeed to judge the social state and political laws of a people.... The most trivial observations of a traveler can lead you to truth on this point as well as the searching remarks of philosophers. Everything goes together in the constitution of moral man as well as in his physical nature, and just as Cuvier, by seeing a single organ, was able to reconstruct the whole body of the entire animal, someone who would know one of the opinions or habits of a people would often be able, I think, to conceive a fairly complete picture of the people itself."[21]

In his writings, Tocqueville repeatedly pointed out examples of such telling details, from the democratic handshake among Americans committed to their presumed social equality, to the warm affection expressed among brothers or between fathers and sons of increasingly democratic families, or to the types of poetry, literature, and public monuments preferred by democratic nations. Two such revealing specifics cited by Tocqueville are especially well known. Perhaps thinking of his own marriage to Mary Mottley, he remarked both in the second part of *Democracy in America* (1840) and in *The Old Regime* (1856) that marriage between spouses of different classes is a clear marker of advancing democracy.[22] In *The Old Regime* he also pointed to the expanded meaning of the word *gentleman* as an indication of the decline of aristocratic caste. The history of the term, he declared, "is the history of democracy itself."[23]

Tocqueville's use of such details not only demonstrated his broader social and political theory, but also served as a useful technique for captivating his readers and persuading them of the soundness of his analysis. In drafts for *The Old Regime* he reminded himself: "Make an effort to avoid as much as possible, in all these chapters, the abstract style, in order to make myself fully understood, and above all, read with pleasure. Make a constant effort to contain abstract and general ideas in words which present a precise and particular picture."[24] The right detail, Tocqueville realized, could seal his argument. And who would not be fascinated by the well-chosen snapshot or revealing observation?

Rejection of Absolutes

We have already noted Tocqueville's view that few certainties or absolutes exist; human beings could at best attain *almosts*. During his American journey, he confided to Ernest de Chabrol: "The more I examine this country and everything, the more I see and the more I am frightened by seeing the few certainties that man is able to acquire in the world. There is no subject that does not grow larger as you pursue it, no fact or observation at the bottom of which you do not find a doubt.... I would like to hold political and moral truths as I hold my pen, and doubt besieges me."[25]

But this world of probabilities troubled him. "There is another intellectual sickness," he wrote to Royer-Collard, "that also torments me constantly. This is an unrestrained and unreasonable passion for certainty.... I persist in the pursuit of an empty shadow that escapes me every day and, not grasping it, I cannot console myself."[26]

If certainty was unattainable, Tocqueville at least hoped to avoid complete relativism. In drafts of the second volume of *Democracy in America*, he wrote: "It is necessary to find in some part of the work ... the ideas of the *middle* that has been so dishonored in our times. Show that there is a firm, clear, voluntary way to see and to grasp the truth between two extremes. To conceive and to say that the truth is not in an absolute system.... Dare to say ... that a difference must be made between absolute affirmation [on the one hand] and Pyrrhonism [or skepticism, on the other], that a system of probabilities is the only true one, the only *human* one, provided that probability causes you to act as energetically as certitude. All that is poorly said, but the germ is there."[27]

For Tocqueville, two especially significant corollaries followed from the rejection of absolutes. First, he refused to accept deterministic systems. Perhaps his best-known and fullest statement of this principle appears in the chapter from the 1840 *Democracy* entitled "Of Some Tendencies Particular to Historians in Democratic Centuries." There he denounced the habit of system making, condemning historical explanations that focused on vast, general causes; or stressed materialistic explanations, such as physical situation or race, or vague causes, such as the spirit of civilization; or linked events and facts together by a tight and necessary chain, falling into a doctrine of fatality.

The consequences of such ideas were lamentable. "A cause vast enough to be applied at the same time to millions of men, and strong enough to bend all of them in the same direction, easily seems irresistible.... So historians who live in democratic times... take away from peoples themselves the ability to modify their own fate, and subject them either to an inflexible providence or to a sort of blind fatality.... You would say, while surveying the histories written in our time, that man can do nothing either for himself or around him.... I will say, moreover, that such a doctrine [of fatality] is particularly dangerous in this period in which we live."[28]

Rejecting materialist as well as fatalistic doctrines also led Tocqueville to an explicit and powerful repudiation of theories of racial inequality. Here was the second important consequence of his stance on deterministic systems. He had definitively abandoned such ideas while traveling in the United States, and, from 1831 onward, his views remained constant.[29] In the 1835 *Democracy*, he denounced not only slavery and the efforts of some Americans to justify the peculiar institution on grounds of racial inferiority, but also the underlying disease of American racism.[30] And in a famous exchange of letters in 1853 with his friend Arthur de Gobineau, who had written an early book upholding the doctrine of racial inequality, Tocqueville laid out the reasons for his rejection of all ideas about superior and inferior races and concluded: "Do you not see that your doctrine brings out naturally all the evils that permanent inequality creates – pride, violence, the contempt of fellow men, tyranny, and abjectness under all its forms? ... We are separated by too great a space for discussion to be fruitful. There is an intellectual world between your doctrine and mine."[31] In later chapters, we will examine the complicated connections between Tocqueville's laudatory ideas about racial equality and his more nuanced attitudes about abolition, colonization, and imperialism.

His rejection of determinism left attentive readers and Tocqueville himself with a problem. Wasn't the providential advance of democracy predetermined and inevitable? In drafts for the 1840 *Democracy*, he wrote: "Idea of necessity, of fatality.... Explain how my system is perfectly compatible with human liberty.... You have not reproached me as I anticipated for seeming to fall into the *mania* of the century. But I reproach myself for it because I do not want to fall into it. You absolve me, and I accuse myself."[32] But the only explanation ultimately provided by Tocqueville appeared in the concluding paragraphs of the book: "I am not unaware that several of my contemporaries have thought that here below peoples are never masters of themselves, and that they obey necessarily I do not know what insurmountable and unintelligent force that arises from previous events, from race, from soil, or from climate. Those are false and cowardly doctrines that can produce only weak men and pusillanimous nations. Providence has created humanity neither entirely independent nor completely slave. It traces around each man, it is true, a fatal circle out of which he cannot go; but within its vast limits, man is powerful and free; so are peoples."[33] Was this effort to find the middle ground and to escape his own brand of fatalism sufficient? His readers are left to judge.

The Right of Property

Yet another bedrock principle for Tocqueville was the right of property. In the section from the 1835 *Democracy* entitled "Of the Idea of Rights in the United States," he explained why complaints against property, growing in Europe, were absent in America. Property ownership was widespread in the "country of democracy par excellence.... Each person, having an individual possession to defend, recognizes in principle the right of property."[34] The implication, perhaps counter-intuitive to some French critics of democracy, was that equality of conditions could strengthen respect for property rights.

Tocqueville's commitment to this principle only strengthened over the next two decades. In an address made in Normandy in 1848, he responded to the events of the February Revolution that ended the July Monarchy and to the increasing attacks on property by socialist theorists. He reminded his fellow citizens that republican govern-ment meant "the rule of the rights of each guaranteed by the will of all; it is genuine respect for all kinds of legitimate property." He again cited the United States as proof.[35]

One of his most impassioned defenses of private property came in yet another speech, delivered in September 1848, in which he opposed a proposal to oblige the government to provide work for all able-bodied citizens. In his remarks, Tocqueville focused on the larger question of socialism, asking "whether the February Revolution is or is not a socialist revolution." His critique of socialist ideas was broad and fierce; one of his central points emphasized the way in which socialism undermined "the very principles of individual property." "The French Revolution," he argued, "waged a cruel, energetic war against some proprietors, but as for the principle of private property itself, it always respected and honored it." Once again, he provided the example of America, "the only truly democratic republic known to history," where property rights were not doubted.[36] And in his Foreword to the twelfth edition of *Democracy in America*, also in 1848, he declared: "It remains for us to learn if we will have ... a Republic that threatens the sacred rights of property ... or a Republic that acknowledges and consecrates them."[37] Such quasi-religious language about property is remarkable from a theorist famous for his eloquent words about "the holy cult of liberty."[38]

The Old Regime repeated much the same message about property rights. The germs of socialism, including the lamentable concept of the "community of goods," were already present, Tocqueville argued, in the ideas of various reformers during the decades before the French Revolution. And he even accused the French government itself of teaching contempt for private property to the people in the eighteenth century.[39] His attachment to the principle of property rights serves as an excellent example of a lifelong belief that not only endured in his writings, but also moved, during the last decade of his life, into a far more central and emotional place in his thinking.

Why such fidelity to the principle of private property? As we will see, Tocqueville strongly preferred a system of numerous small-holdings as opposed to fewer large estates. What benefits did he ascribe to widespread property ownership? For him, owning property meant not only a guard against poverty, but also greater individual independence, the creation of social bonds among property owners, and the development of a distinct mentality, of habits or mores that encouraged moderation and an orderly society. These social characteristics all served as remedies for potential democratic dangers.

Perhaps most fundamentally, he thought the right of private property essential to civilization itself. Even here, however, he shied away from absolutes. "I have no doubt that the laws that constitute our modern society will in the long run be subject to many modifications. ... The more I study what the world used to be like, and the more I learn in detail about the world of today, when I consider the prodigious diversity one finds in it, not only in regard to laws but also in regard to the principles that underlie the laws and the different forms that the right of property has taken and continues to exhibit today, ... I am tempted to believe that what some call necessary institutions are often only the institutions to which we are accustomed, and that when it comes to the constitution of society, the realm of the possible is far wider than the people who live in any particular society imagine."[40]

Impartiality and Moderation

Tocqueville's preference for the middle between complete doubt and absolute certainty reflected a broader intellectual impulse. He wanted to be a man of no particular party, to stand apart from easy political classification. His Introduction to the 1835 *Democracy* concluded: "I finish by pointing out myself what a great number of readers will consider as the capital defect of the work. This book follows in no one's train exactly; by writing it I did not mean either to serve or to combat any party; I set about to see, not differently, but farther than parties; and while they are concerned with the next day, I wanted to think about the future."[41] This desire to remain impartial amounted to another of Tocqueville's first principles.

In 1837, in a letter to Henry Reeve, his English translator, he declared: "It delights me to see the different features that are given to me according to the political passions of the person who cites me. ... They absolutely want to make me a party man and I am not that in the least; they assign to me passions and I have only opinions, or rather I have only one passion, the love of liberty and human dignity." He went on to explain his ability to find middle ground. "I came into the world at the end of a long Revolution, which, after having destroyed the old state, had created nothing durable. Aristocracy was already dead when I started life and democracy did not yet exist, so my instinct could lead me blindly neither toward one nor toward the other." He described himself as "thoroughly in equilibrium between the past and the future."[42]

In drafts of *The Old Regime*, Tocqueville admitted the consequences of his position with remarkable honesty. "I am alone. This isolation in the middle of my country is often cruel. Feeling the pain, I wanted at least to taste the corresponding pleasure, which is to express my thoughts freely, without wishing to flatter, without fearing to displease, concerning myself with the truth alone."[43]

Despite these words, Tocqueville always took care not to displease his audience, at least unnecessarily. His stance of impartiality lent a tone of moderation not only to most of his social and political views, but also to his language. As the many revisions to the drafts for both *Democracy in America* and *The Old Regime* make clear, he worked as a writer to excise overly emotional words or passages and excessively provocative opinions from his final texts. The constant goal was to persuade his readers as gently and effectively as possible and not to turn them away with hard pronouncements. The exception that proves Tocqueville's rule is, of course, his *Recollections*, which he intended to be published only after his death. There he included biting portraits, intense emotions, uncensored comments, and unrestrained judgments. His posthumous book stands as least characteristic of his habitual moderation of position, tone, and language.

Tocqueville's claims of impartiality were, in some ways, genuine, reflecting his sense of being apart from his own times and outside the usual political camps. But his neutrality was also more than a bit exaggerated; it remained something of a pose to reassure and capture his audience. On some matters he remained unyielding.

Concluding Comments: Tocqueville the Moralist

Our brief review has highlighted several of Tocqueville's most enduring underlying beliefs, such as: the march of democracy; the idea of three causes and the primacy of mores; the multifaceted and complex nature of any society; the rejection of determinism, materialism, and racism; the right of property; and the search for moderation and the middle ground. It has also explained a few of his key terms – including *idée mère* (mother idea), point of departure, social state, circumstances, laws, and mores – and revealed some of his habitual ways of thinking and writing, especially his inclination to revisit ideas and to leave definitions open-ended. As we move ahead, we will explore other themes and concepts essential to Tocqueville's thinking and writing. But perhaps a unifying thread has already emerged.

Tocqueville repeatedly affirmed his unwavering attachment to liberty and human dignity. As a student of Pascal, he strove always to uphold the human spirit and enlarge the human soul. Throughout his life, he defended the ability of human beings to shape their own destiny and insisted on their responsibility to participate in the great venture of preserving liberty in the democratic age. This moral enterprise linked his efforts as an author and political figure and served as his most essential purpose as a theorist.

3

Major Themes: Equality, Democracy, Liberty, and Revolution

Equality

We now come to the heart of Tocqueville's social and political theory, the meanings in his thinking and writing of the words equality, democracy, liberty, and revolution. Tocqueville opened his book in 1835 with a bow to *equality of conditions* as the "central point where all my observations came together," and then moved into a discussion of advancing democracy and the great democratic revolution.[1] Despite a failure to reach definitive definitions, Tocqueville never lost the impulse to clarify his terms.

Perhaps the earliest effort to explain his sense of equality appears in a letter written from the New World to Louis de Kergorlay in June 1831. Near the beginning of his epistle, Tocqueville remarked on the basic education widely shared by Americans (their enlightenment), and then, in following paragraphs, presented other essential elements of the equality of conditions that prevailed in the United States.

Americans had started out equal by many measures, but Tocqueville explained to his friend how changes since the American Revolution in the laws of land inheritance had accelerated equality of conditions in the New World republic. He stressed the division of landed estates, the decline of the class of great landowners, the loss of family spirit, and the end of any aristocratic tendency. The consequences were unmistakable. In the United States, property changed hands rapidly, landownership was widespread, and equality of wealth increased. Rapid change (even instability) and mobility marked the entire nation. These social and economic features were accompanied by "an external equality," "a tone of manners," and "a uniformly common turn of ideas."[2] In his missive, he also pointed out that to have a healthy society, egalitarian civil laws need to be matched by similar political laws. Tocqueville specifically cited broad electoral rights in the American republic, where equality in the political world was in harmony with equality in the social and economic realms. He would insist on this general principle in one of his notes for the 1840 *Democracy*: "[In] the long run, political society cannot fail to become the expression and the image of civil society."[3]

Tocqueville carried most of his discussion with Kergorlay directly into the pages of the third chapter of the 1835 *Democracy*, entitled "Social State of the Anglo-Americans," where he further explained the importance of inheritance laws and repeated his catalogue of the varieties of equality.[4] His depiction of the American republic as a society characterized by equality of conditions included: (1) material and economic equality – a general level of comfort and material well-being; rough equality of wealth; widespread property ownership; economic mobility, with fortunes and families constantly rising and falling; the decline of hereditary wealth; and a significant degree of economic opportunity; (2) social and psychological equality – similar manners and mores; a relatively open society with no fixed classes (social mobility); the expectation of mutual respect and esteem; a level of social ease among classes; the decline of deference; and a sense of being equal to others (despite tangible inequalities);[5] (3) intellectual equality – shared basic education and a general level of middling knowledge; similar ideas, opinions and beliefs; and (4) political equality – the right to vote and to participate in the political world – as well as other basic political and civil rights.

Tocqueville was not blind to contrary features; in his travel diaries, as well as in the drafts and published text of the 1835 *Democracy*, he recognized some of the inequalities that existed in the American republic.[6] What he described in his chapter on social state applied, as he said, to Anglo-Americans, not to other races in the United States; African Americans, both slave and free, and Native Americans were not included in this view of equality. And some elements of his portrait of American equality did not include women of any race. In addition, his research on the penitentiary system made him aware of economic inequalities and the problem of poverty in the United States. Despite his stress on American equality, he would not entirely forget these contrasting, non-egalitarian traits.

Tocqueville completed his description of American equality by posing a dilemma that would constantly resurface in his writings, serving as a kind of subtext in all his musings about the future of democratic societies. "The political consequences of such [an egalitarian] social state are easy to deduce. It is impossible to think that, in the end, equality would not penetrate the political world as it does elsewhere.... Now I know only two ways to have equality rule in the political world: rights must either be given to each citizen or given to no one.... For peoples who have arrived at the same social state as the Anglo-Americans, it is therefore very difficult to see a middle course between the sovereignty of all [sovereignty of the people] and the absolute power of one man.... Peoples can therefore draw two great political consequences from the same social state; these consequences differ prodigiously; but they both arise from the same fact." Given the "fearful alternative" of liberty or despotism faced by all democratic societies, the Anglo-Americans were "fortunate enough to escape absolute power."[7] But what destiny awaited France and other nations? Here was one of Tocqueville's central questions as a theorist.

In 1838, as he drafted the second volume of *Democracy*, Tocqueville returned to the definition of equality, but with no specific reference to the American example. "In Preface, I believe. Explain somewhere what I understand by centuries of equality. It is not that chimerical time when all men will be perfectly similar and equal, but those: 1. When a great number among them will ... fall either above or below, but not far from the common measure. 2. Those when there will be no more permanent classification, caste, class, any insurmountable barrier or even one very difficult to surmount, so that if all men are not equal, they can all aspire to the same point; some ... to fear falling, others to hope to rise, so that a common measure makes itself [felt?] against which all men measure themselves in advance, which spreads the sentiment of equality even within unequal conditions."[8] Here, Tocqueville again stressed social and economic mobility, shared aspirations and anxieties, and the psychological sense of equality, even in the face of actual inequalities. Perhaps the concept of an open society, where nothing is fixed and everything is in motion, serves as the single most essential characteristic of Tocqueville's understanding of equality of conditions.

In the pages of *The Old Regime*, Tocqueville's description of equality was even more general. He simply asserted the passage toward democratic equality. France during the eighteenth century, he argued, was moving toward a kind of social and economic equality, marked by the decline, even the destruction, of the aristocracy, the rise of the middle class, and the broadening of landownership. French society witnessed a growing hatred for remaining inequalities, rising aspirations, and the wide embrace of an ideology that insisted on the equality of all human beings.[9] But no movement toward political equality accompanied this tendency toward a degree of social, economic, psychological, and intellectual equality. Tocqueville pronounced this disjuncture potentially explosive.

By the early 1840s, his definition of equality took on some new dimensions, an expansion rooted in his understanding of the origins of the idea of equality. The concept drew its source, he believed, from Christianity. For him, one of the remarkable features of the Christian religion was its insistence on the equality of all human beings. "All the great writers of antiquity," he observed in the 1840 *Democracy*, "were part of the aristocracy of masters, or at least they saw this aristocracy established without dispute before their eyes;...Jesus Christ had to come to earth in order to make it understood that all members of the human species were naturally similar and equal."[10]

He had already made the same assertion in the manuscript of his subchapter on "Religion Considered as a Political Institution" in the United States, from the 1835 *Democracy*. "Of all religious doctrines," he wrote, "Christianity...is also the one most favorable to equality."[11] Tocqueville never abandoned this belief; it reappeared years later in a letter sent to Gobineau in 1857, where he argued that his friend's theory of racial inequality was not only deterministic and materialistic, but also contrary to both the letter and the spirit of the Christian religion. "Christianity...wanted to abolish all distinctions of race...and [to make] only one human species, all of whose members were equally capable of perfecting themselves and of becoming alike.... Christianity," he told Gobineau, "certainly tended to make all men brothers and equals."[12]

Christian principles also helped to push the meaning of equality in new directions. After the publication of the 1840 volume of *Democracy in America*, and perhaps in response to his new role in politics, Tocqueville proposed a more up-to-date twist on the concept of equality. Contemporary morality, he observed in yet another letter to Gobineau, had expanded the traditional Christian perspective on equality to include "the idea that *all* men have a right to certain goods, to certain enjoyments, and that the first moral obligation is to obtain those things for them.... This first innovation led to another: Christianity had made benevolence or...charity a private virtue. We are making it more and more a social duty, a political obligation, a public virtue.... We have imposed [on governments] a strict obligation to rectify certain inequalities, to come to the relief of certain miseries, to offer support to all the weak, to all the unfortunate." This, he declared, is a new "sort of social and political morality."[13]

As we will see, Tocqueville's responses to these recent moral imperatives, especially his ideas about how best to alleviate poverty and to redress extreme inequalities, and his views about the appropriate level of governmental involvement in such activities, were complex, nuanced, and sometimes contradictory. But his consideration of these questions opened the door to a variety of later proposals for reform.

In addition to his exploration of the varieties of equality, Tocqueville wrote often about the passion for equality, which paradoxically grew more intense as inequalities diminished and seemed always to outlast a companion passion for liberty. He first touched on this topic in the 1835 *Democracy*, where he distinguished between a "manly and legitimate passion for equality...[that] tends to elevate the small to the rank of the great" and "a depraved taste for equality...that leads the weak to want to bring the strong down to their level and that reduces men to preferring equality in servitude to inequality in liberty."[14]

This theme persisted in Tocqueville's thinking and would reemerge in a famous chapter from the 1840 *Democracy*, "Why Democratic Peoples Show a More Ardent and More Enduring Love for Equality Than for Liberty." "I think that democratic peoples have a natural taste for liberty; left to themselves, they seek it, they love it, and it is only with pain that they see themselves separated from it. But they have an ardent, insatiable, eternal, invincible passion for equality; they want equality in liberty, and if they cannot obtain that, they still want equality in slavery. They will suffer poverty, enslavement, barbarism, but they will not suffer aristocracy."[15]

Tocqueville's analysis of the dual, but unequal, passions for equality and for liberty also appeared in *The Old Regime*; these twin desires, he explained, were an essential part of the story of the origins and course of the French Revolution. "Those who, in reading this book, have carefully studied eighteenth-century France have been able to see two chief passions born and developed in the nation's breast.... One, deeper and coming from further back, is the violent and inextinguishable hatred of inequality.... The other passion, more recent and less well rooted, brought them to want to live not only equal, but free.

"Towards the end of the old regime these two passions are equally sincere and seem equally lively. At the start of the Revolution they meet; they mix and join for a moment and then, heating each other by contact, finally inflame the whole heart of France at once. This is '89, a time of inexperience doubtless, but of generosity, of enthusiasm, of virility, and of greatness, a time of immortal memory ... [From when the Revolution began down to our own days] the passion for equality has still retained possession of the depths of the hearts that it first conquered.... While the passion for freedom constantly changes its appearance, shrinks, grows, strengthens, and weakens according to events, the passion for equality is always the same, always attached to the same purpose with the same obstinate and often blind ardor, ready to sacrifice everything to those who permit it to satisfy itself, and to furnish to the government willing to favor and flatter it, the habits, ideas and laws that despotism needs in order to rule."[16] (The blunt condemnation of Louis-Napoleon and the Second Empire was unmistakable.)

For Tocqueville, the moment when the two passions for equality and liberty joined provided a fleeting time of incomparable beauty and pride. For him, the spirit of '89 stood as the high point of the French Revolution. The sixty-plus years that followed marked a period of instability and loss. One of his abiding purposes was to explain why this had happened; another was to suggest what might be done.

Democracy

Tocqueville, we have remarked, used the words *equality* (or *equality of conditions*) and *democracy* somewhat interchangeably. The two terms often appear as alternative readings for the same sentence in the drafts of *Democracy in America*. Both concepts, Tocqueville realized, had social and political dimensions. In the margin of the working manuscript for the 1835 volume, where he had attempted to define social state, he also reminded himself: "Explain what is understood by democracy."

In an initial fragment of his chapter on the American social state, he remarked: "As soon as you look at the civil and political society of the United States, you discover two great facts ... *Democracy* constitutes the social state; the dogma of *sovereignty of the people*, the political law. These two things are not analogous. Democracy is society's way of being. Sovereignty of the people, a form of ... government. Nor are they inseparable, because democracy is even more compatible with despotism than with liberty. But they are correlative. Sovereignty of the people is always more or less a fiction wherever democracy is not established."

Tocqueville discarded this early attempt at definition however. He found it misleading, writing in the margin: "Note that in this chapter the social state must never be confused with the political laws that follow from it; equality or inequality of conditions, which are facts, with democracy or aristocracy, which are laws. Reexamine from this point of view."[17] This corrected effort also remained somewhat obscure, but at least he had made an essential distinction. Equality of conditions related primarily to social state; democracy, mostly to laws, especially political laws. In these early drafts, Tocqueville had also stated one of the fundamental points of his social and political analysis: democracy paired more easily with despotism than with liberty. Here perhaps was the most serious and recurring warning in the entire body of his work as a theorist. In the age of democracy, how was liberty to be saved?

In words that strikingly parallel his discussion of equality of conditions, Tocqueville elaborated on the meaning of democracy in another draft from the first volume of his book (1835): "Democracy. What is most important for democracy is not that there are no great fortunes; it is that great fortunes do not rest in the same hands. In this way, there are the rich, but they do not form a class. Commerce, industry perhaps create larger individual fortunes in America now than sixty years ago. [Note Tocqueville's qualification of advancing equality in the United States.] However, the abolition of primogeniture and entail make democracy, its passions, interests, maxims, tastes more powerful in our time than sixty years ago. Furthermore, equality of political rights has introduced a powerful new element of democracy. American societies had always been democratic by their nature; the Revolution made democratic principles pass into the laws."[18] In the 1840 *Democracy*, Tocqueville insisted even more strongly on mobility as an essential feature of democratic nations, where "a type of permanent agitation," "a small, uncomfortable movement," and "a sort of incessant rotation" reign.[19]

In later writings, Tocqueville sketched at least two other specific attempts to define democracy. "What is democracy?" he mused in 1848. "It is giving the greatest possible share of freedom, knowledge and power to all."[20] The second effort, focused on the political world, appeared in his "General Remarks" relating to the incomplete second volume of *The Old Regime*. "*Democracy. Democratic institutions. Various meanings of these words. Confusion that results from this*. What confuses the mind most is the use we make of these words: *democracy, democratic institutions, democratic government*. As long as we do not succeed in defining them clearly and agreeing on the definition, we will live in an incredible confusion of ideas, to the great profit of demagogues and despots. Some will say that a country governed by an absolute ruler is a *democracy*, because he governs through equal laws or amidst institutions that will be favorable to the condition of the lower classes. His government will be a *democratic government*. He will create a *democratic monarchy*.

"But the words *democra[tic] monarchy, democratic government*, in the true sense of those words, can only mean one thing: a government where the people play a more or less large part in the government. Their meaning is intimately linked to the idea of political freedom. To give the name *democratic government* to a government where political freedom is not found is to say a palpable absurdity, according to the natural meaning of the words."[21]

In these reflections Tocqueville once again underscored democracy as related to political laws (in contrast to equality, related to social state). He also posed the issue of popular participation as a hallmark of democracy and wrestled with the question of the legitimate role of democratic government, matters that would continue to be concerns for him throughout the 1840s and 1850s.

Curiously, the word democracy appears infrequently in the text of *The Old Regime*. Tocqueville usually wrote instead about the decline of aristocracy or the development of certain varieties of equality. But always behind his argument hides the inevitable advance of democracy. In 1856, he seemed to be describing eighteenth-century France as a case study in the particular dangers of democracy when it comes without political liberty.

Tocqueville's ongoing examination of the meanings of democracy, of its potential benefits and dangers, reveals another of his fundamental purposes. In 1835, he wrote to his friend Francisque de Corcelle that he aimed toward "the progressive organization of democracy," adding: "I sought... to establish what the natural tendencies were that a democratic social state gave to the spirit and institutions of man. I pointed out the dangers that awaited humanity on this path. But I did not pretend that one could not struggle against these tendencies, uncovered and resisted in time, that one could not avert these dangers foreseen in advance. It seemed to me that the Democrats (and I take this word in its good sense), that the Democrats of our time, I say, saw clearly neither the advantages nor the dangers of the social and political state toward which they sought to lead society and that consequently they were in danger of being mistaken about the means to use to make the first as large as possible and the second as small as can be. So I undertook to show all of them [advantages and dangers], clearly and with all the strength of which I am capable, in order that you see your enemies face to face and know what you are fighting against."[22] As he said in a draft for the 1840 *Democracy*, "I am profoundly convinced that democracy can be regulated and organized; it is not something easy, but it is something that can be done, and I add that it is the only thing left to do."[23] This purpose in a nutshell fit *The Old Regime* as well.

Yet another way to understand *democracy* was to examine *aristocracy* as a foil. Tocqueville's journeys to England in 1833 and 1835 launched an ongoing consideration of the particular characteristics of the English aristocracy and of the different possible types of aristocracy – English, Irish, and French.[24] This extended examination would find forceful expression in *The Old Regime* where Tocqueville contrasted a healthy English aristocracy, resistant to revolution, relatively open, and deeply involved in the political world, and an eighteenth-century French aristocracy, closed to the point of becoming a caste, completely disengaged from political life (even parasitic), and ripe for destruction.

And much of the second volume of *Democracy in America* may be read as a series of contrasting portraits of aristocratic and democratic societies, as a study of opposing ideal types. For Tocqueville, aristocracy at its best meant great landed estates held over generations, ties of mutual obligation up and down the social ladder, important individuals or families that could act as centers of independence and resistance, and a class with the leisure to provide political, cultural, and intellectual leadership. In his 1840 text, he constantly moved from descriptions of the intellectual, artistic, cultural, social, emotional, economic, and political affinities of aristocracies to those of democracies. Even in his 1835 work, he had at least once put the opposing characteristics of aristocratic and democratic nations side by side and asked his readers to choose what kind of society they preferred.[25] Much like the art of making silhouettes, outlining aristocracy could reveal the characteristic features of democracy.

Tocqueville insisted that he wrote both *Democracy in America* and *The Old Regime* as an impartial observer and commentator. Where did he stand on democracy? His position was elusive, and his comments often contradictory. To John Stuart Mill, he asserted in June 1835: "I love liberty by taste, equality by instinct and reason. These two passions, which so many pretend to have, I am convinced that I really feel in myself, and that I am prepared to make great sacrifices for them." After contrasting the dangerous French democrats with their English counterparts, he praised the latter and concluded: "At least theirs is the true goal that friends of Democracy must take. Their final object seems to me to be, in reality, to put the majority of citizens in a fit state for governing and to make it capable of governing. ... I am myself a democrat in this sense."[26]

A few months earlier, Tocqueville had explained the political goal of his recent book to Eugène Stoffels. "I tried to show ... that if democratic governments developed less than some other governments certain beautiful faculties of the human soul, it had beautiful and grand sides; and that perhaps, after all, the will of God was to diffuse a mediocre happiness on the totality of men, and not to concentrate a large amount of felicity on some and allow only a small number to approach perfection."[27] These words foreshadowed passages that would occur in the final chapter of the 1840 *Democracy*, where Tocqueville summarized eloquently: "It is natural to believe that what most satisfies the sight of [the] creator and preserver of men, is not the singular prosperity of a few, but the greatest well-being of all; so what seems to me decline, is in his eyes progress; what hurts me, agrees with him. Equality is perhaps less elevated; but it is more just, and its justice makes its grandeur and its beauty. I try hard to enter into this point of view of God, and from there I seek to consider and to judge human things."[28]

"You see," Tocqueville declared in discarded drafts of his 1840 book, "that my tendencies are always democratic. I am a partisan of democracy without having any illusion about its faults and without failing to recognize its dangers. I am even all the more so as I believe that I see both more clearly, because I am profoundly convinced that there is no way to prevent its triumph, and that it is only by marching with it and by directing its progress as much as possible that you can decrease the evils it brings and produce the good things that it promises."[29]

But other fragments remain more ambiguous. In about 1841, he wrote: "Let us ... sincerely look for *my fundamental instincts* and *my serious principles*. I have an intellectual preference for democratic institutions, but I am aristocratic by instinct, that is I despise and fear the crowd. I passionately love freedom, legality, the respect for rights, but not democracy. This is the base of my soul. I hate demagogy, the disorderly action of the masses, their violent and uneducated participation in affairs, the lower classes' envious passions, the irreligious tendencies. This is the base of my soul. ... Freedom is the first of my passions. This is what is true."[30] This frank admission of instincts and principles touches on Tocqueville's love of liberty; his drive to prepare, educate, and moderate the people; and his hatred, as we will see, for what he called the spirit of revolution. As for Tocqueville's position on democracy, we are left with the impression, on the one hand, of a rational acceptance and a determination to make the best of what could not be escaped, and, on the other, of a quasi-religious assent to following a different path to beauty and justice in human affairs.

Liberty

How are equality, democracy, and liberty related? If equality and democracy, in Tocqueville's thinking and writing, were often transposable and sometimes distinguishable only with difficulty, the same was emphatically not true about democracy and liberty. Tocqueville acknowledged an instinctive love of freedom among democratic peoples, but for him democracy led more easily to despotism than to liberty. And if true liberty in democratic societies required at least a moderate level of equality, liberty and equality remained two unequal passions.

These judgments need to be kept in mind by today's readers of Tocqueville; we tend to conflate democracy with freedom and see equality and liberty as two sides of the same coin. Tocqueville did not make these mistakes. For him, as we have seen, democracy put liberty at risk. As a man of theory and action, he wanted to explain the meaning and importance of liberty, to show how it could counteract the dangers of democracy, and to suggest how liberty might be protected in democratic times.

Tocqueville considered liberty the highest moral value. "As always," he confided in a letter written in 1856 to Madame Swetchine, "I consider freedom to be the greatest of goods. I still see freedom as one of the most fertile sources of manly virtues and great actions."[31] He called it "a *sacred* thing" and, as we have already noted, declared it "the first of my passions."[32]

"I have often wondered," he wrote in *The Old Regime*, "where the source of this passion for political freedom is.... [What], in all times, has so strongly attached certain men's hearts to freedom, are its own attractions, its own peculiar charm, independent of its benefits; it is the pleasure of being able to speak, act, and breathe without constraint, under the government of God and the laws alone. Whoever seeks for anything from freedom but itself is made for slavery.... Do not ask me to analyze this sublime desire [to be free]; it must be felt. It enters of itself into the great hearts that God has prepared to receive it; it fills them, it fires them. One must give up on making this comprehensible to the mediocre souls who have never felt it."[33] Tocqueville's language about liberty recalls descriptions of religious conversion or the coming of divine grace.

But for Tocqueville, liberty was not simply, or even primarily, an abstract moral concept; it evoked an array of specific liberties. In both *Democracy in America* and *The Old Regime*, as well as in many of his other essays and addresses, Tocqueville often defined liberty by enumerating a variety of particular freedoms and guarantees. A free society, he argued, required a package of many basic civil and political rights, such as the right to vote, freedom of expression (including freedom of speech and freedom of the press), and the rights of association and assembly; these were essential for genuine participation in public life. He also recommended an independent judiciary, trial by jury, local and provincial liberties, property rights, protection of the freedom of the individual person, and separation of church and state; such institutional arrangements would leave room for the assertion of independence and resistance to any potential despotism.

Tocqueville's listings of these liberties are scattered throughout his writings. In at least two places, however, he presented important summaries that are useful to consult. The first appeared in the penultimate chapter of the 1840 *Democracy*, entitled "Continuation of Preceding Chapters."[34] The second, less familiar, was delivered in an address to the Academy of Moral and Political Sciences in January 1848. In his speech, Tocqueville reviewed and strongly criticized a recent study of democracy in Switzerland. He argued that the Swiss, far from being democratic, still lacked the freedoms essential for what he called "modern liberty."[35] He decided to include his remarks on Switzerland as an Appendix in the twelfth edition of *Democracy in America* published in 1848. In addition, we should note the defense of provincial liberties offered by Tocqueville in his discussion of the province of Languedoc, also included as an Appendix, this time in *The Old Regime*. Languedoc, where "local life was still active," served him as a kind of alternative possible history, an example of "what might have been" in eighteenth-century France if public life had not been gradually smothered.[36]

In Tocqueville's analysis, neither liberty as an abstract value nor liberties as specific legal and institutional protections are simply bestowed. A free society meant not only having the required cluster of rights, but also putting those rights to use. One of his most important themes is what he called the *practice of liberty*. By this term,

Tocqueville understood both a kind of training or apprenticeship in freedom and the actual *doing* or experience of liberty. For example, the practice of local self-government formed the capacity for self-government on the larger, national stage. And exercising the rights to vote, associate, assemble, speak, and write led to effective public participation and civic engagement. Liberty, for Tocqueville, is made real by rights in action.

From another perspective, Tocqueville was describing two kinds of liberty. First were the basic civil and political rights noted above; these provided the essential preconditions of freedom. Such necessary rights had to be real, not hollow; they set the stage for genuine liberty. Second, and perhaps more fundamental in his thinking, was the exercise of liberty, putting these required preconditions into use. This view of true liberty as involvement in public life distinguished Tocqueville from many of his contemporary theorists.

So the *practice of liberty* implied not the passive or negative liberty of simply being left alone by the government or other centers of social power, but an active or positive liberty. True freedom meant not merely the absence of constraint, but the actual use of rights, immersion in civic life, and participation in public affairs. Tocqueville dismissed as false any liberty that consisted of legal forms without substance. The right to vote, for example, meant nothing if you could not cast your ballot, or if, lacking any viable opposition, you had no real choice to make. The freedom to assemble rang hollow if places of assembly were routinely unavailable for public gatherings. In his Preface to *The Old Regime*, he pointedly condemned the false liberty of the Empire and Napoleon. "I will show how this government called the votes of electors who could neither inform themselves, nor organize, nor choose, 'the sovereignty of the people.'"[37] For Tocqueville, liberty required the ongoing exercise and experience of rights; an empty show of freedom did not qualify.

In 1836, he wrote to Eugène Stoffels: "I think that … the majority of the nation itself can be involved with its own affairs, that political life can be spread almost everywhere, the direct or indirect exercise of political rights can be quite extensive. … As for the means: with all those who admit that we must make our way gradually toward this goal, I am very much in accord. I am the first to admit that it is necessary to proceed slowly, with caution, with legality. … I wish that the government would itself prepare mores and practices …. I wish that citizens were introduced into public life to the extent that they are believed capable of being useful in it, instead of seeking to keep them away from it at all costs."[38] These remarks echo his words, already noted, to John Stuart Mill about working "to put the majority of citizens in a fit state for governing."[39] They also underscore his instinct for moderation and his gradualist approach. We will return to these characteristics of Tocqueville's thinking when we look at his political program.

Some nations enjoyed a long experience in the exercise of freedom. *Democracy in America*, of course, presented the American example to readers; Tocqueville especially praised the practical political experience and impulse for public involvement that characterized the New World republicans. And *The Old Regime* included pointed comparisons of English experience and French inexperience with free institutions. A key thesis of this 1856 work centered on the relentless decay of the exercise of liberty during the 1700s in France. After his third visit across the Channel in 1857, Tocqueville continued his argument; he commented on the marked decline in democratic, even revolutionary, ferment in England, and told Kergorlay: "There is not a single one of my theoretical ideas on the practice of political liberty and on what allows it to function among men that does not seem to me fully justified once again by everything I have been seeing before me."[40] His primary lament was that if England provided a grand spectacle of how best to manage public affairs and prepare men for civic participation, France offered instead a sad contrasting image. Only the reintroduction and actual use of necessary particular liberties appeared to offer a path to freedom for French society and politics in the nineteenth century.

In later chapters we will examine in more detail how freedom, once rooted (or re-rooted) in the institutions and mores of a people, served to maximize the benefits and minimize the dangers of democracy. In both of his major works, however, Tocqueville also described the more general benefits of liberty. The 1856 text of *The Old Regime* repeats an argument that had already appeared in the second volume of *Democracy in America*.[41] Uncertainties, disorders, and even excesses sometimes obscured the advantages of liberty, but, in the end, it alone produced outstanding men and prosperous nations. "At no other times in my life," he told Francisque de Corcelle in 1852, not long after Louis-Napoleon's *coup d'état* and the establishment of the Second Empire, "have I been more personally convinced of the need and superiority of free institutions. I have never seen more clearly that a people does not have real moral greatness without them."[42]

Only a few years after this letter, he developed this point in a passage from the Preface to *The Old Regime*. "Liberty alone can effectively combat the natural vices of [democratic] societies and prevent them from sliding down the slippery slope where they find themselves. Only freedom can bring citizens out of the isolation in which the very independence of their circumstances has led them to live, can daily force them to mingle, to join together through the need to communicate with one another, persuade each other, and satisfy each other in the conduct of their common affairs. Only freedom can tear people from the worship of Mammon and the petty daily concerns of their personal affairs and teach them to always see and feel the nation above and beside them; only freedom can substitute higher and stronger passions for the love of material well-being, give rise to greater ambitions than the acquisition of a fortune....

"Democratic societies that are not free can be wealthy, refined, even splendid, powerful because of the weight of their homogeneous mass; one can find there private virtues, good family men, honest merchants, and very worthy squires.... But what will never exist in such societies are great citizens, and above all a great people.... This is what I said and thought twenty years ago [in the 1835 *Democracy*]. Since then nothing has happened to make me change my mind."[43] Tocqueville demanded liberty in order to cure the social isolation, materialism, and lack of public virtues that not only had gnawed at eighteenth-century France, but also continued to blight the world he saw around him in the 1850s.

For Tocqueville, freedom as a moral force meant an ordered, measured liberty. Probably his most famous statement of this view occurred in the second chapter of the 1835 *Democracy* about the American point of departure. There he named religion as the necessary restraint on the social and political innovations of the New England Puritans and praised the "beautiful definition of liberty" offered by John Winthrop, perennial Governor of the Massachusetts colony. In Tocqueville's words, Winthrop condemned a liberty "which consists of doing whatever you please," but defended "a civil and moral liberty." "It is the liberty," the Governor declared, "to do...all that is just and good. This holy liberty we must defend at all cost...."[44] What Winthrop upheld was freedom limited by morality, by justice and goodness, liberty moderated by religious beliefs. "I have already said enough," Tocqueville summarized in the 1835 *Democracy*, "to reveal Anglo-American civilization in its true light. It is the product (and this point of departure must always be kept in mind) of two perfectly distinct elements that elsewhere are often at odds. But in America, these two have been successfully blended, in a way, and marvelously combined. I mean the *spirit of religion* and the *spirit of liberty*."[45] We will say more in later chapters about the special role of religion in democratic society.

Tocqueville's conviction that liberty needed to adapt to an unavoidable democratic future, and his insistence that liberty required the moral restraints of religion, help to explain both his call for a new political science[46] and his self-identification as a liberal of a new kind. To his friend Eugène Stoffels, he declared in 1836: "What has always struck me about my country...has been to see lined up on one side the men who prize morality, religion, order, and on the other those who love freedom and the equality of men before the law. This sight has struck me as the most extraordinary and most deplorable ever offered a man's view; for all these things, which we separate, are, I am certain, indissolubly united in the eyes of God. They are all holy things.... I have realized that one of the most beautiful enterprises of our times would be to show that all these things are not at all incompatible; that on the contrary, they are necessarily linked to one another.... This is my general idea.... I will therefore show frankly the taste for freedom, and the general desire to see it develop in all the political institutions of my country; but at the same time I will profess such a great respect for justice and religious beliefs, that I can't believe people won't clearly recognize me for *a liberal of a new kind*."[47] In all his writings and actions, Tocqueville hoped to bring men of good will together and end the needless conflict that existed in France between the proponents of liberty and the defenders of religion. His instincts suggested that political moderation and restrained liberty would be the best path forward.

In February 1858, only about a year before the end of his life, Tocqueville wrote to Beaumont: "I do not need to tell you...how much I agree with you...on the value of liberty.... But how difficult it is to establish liberty solidly among people who have lost the practice of it, and even the correct notion of it. What greater impotence than that of institutions, when ideas and mores do not nourish them! I have always believed that the endeavor of making France a free nation (in the true sense of the word), that this endeavor, to which...we have consecrated our lives...was noble and bold."[48] These few words capture the essence of what liberty meant to him: moral value, required practice, and the need for unrelenting effort, by a liberal of a new kind, to assure freedom in democratic times.

Revolution

Tocqueville often thought in terms of opposing pairs, such as liberty and equality, or democracy and aristocracy. Another such pair in tension involved democracy and revolution. It is tempting to separate

Tocqueville's two great works with that duality in mind and to present his book on America as a study of democracy (with little comment on revolution) and *The Old Regime* as a reflection on revolution. From that perspective, the focus of Tocqueville's social and political theory changed dramatically from 1835 to 1856, shifting from democracy to revolution. Such an approach would be a great error, however. Revolution was not a topic that came late to Tocqueville's attention. The very idea of it resurrected lifelong personal and familial memories. From the beginning of *Democracy in America*, where he described "a great democratic revolution," the theme of revolution appeared repeatedly; and he did not write a page of *The Old Regime* without thinking of the coming of democracy.

Tocqueville argued (somewhat incorrectly) in his 1835 book that the United States had experienced no true revolution, only a war of independence. The absence of a revolutionary past eased the task of capturing the image of democracy. "In Europe," he observed, "we have difficulty judging the true character and permanent instincts of democracy, because in Europe there is a struggle between two opposite principles. And we do not know precisely what should be attributed to the principles themselves or to the passions that the conflict has produced. It is not the same in America.... That is where [democracy] must be judged."[49] For Europeans, the collision between the old order and the new society obscured the view of the future.

Repeatedly in the 1840 *Democracy*, Tocqueville asked why the United States was so often exempt from some of the worst consequences of democracy. In addition to favorable circumstances, institutions, and mores, including the long practice of liberty, he asserted that the absence of revolutionary passions explained much of American success. "The great advantage of the Americans," he declared in his text, "is to have arrived at democracy without having to suffer democratic revolutions. And to have been born equal instead of becoming so."

In a related draft, he elaborated: "Effects of democracy, and particularly harmful effects that are exaggerated in the period of revolution when the democratic social state, mores, and laws become established.... The great difficulty in the study of democracy is to distinguish what is democratic from what is only revolutionary. This is very difficult because examples are lacking. There is no European people among whom democracy has settled down, and America is in an exceptional situation. The state of literature in France is not only democratic, but revolutionary. Public morality, id. Religious opinions, id. Political opinions, id."[50] The mutual effects of democracy and revolution were complicated, he realized; democracy could not escape coloration (or discoloration) by revolution.

Notice that in these passages, Tocqueville was thinking about two separate revolutions: the democratic revolution, at work in the world for several hundred years, and the French Revolution, which began in 1789. But he recognized from the outset that the two were intimately linked and that the second was embedded in the first. "While I had my eyes fixed on America, I thought about Europe. I thought about this immense social revolution that is coming to completion among us while we are still discussing its legitimacy and its rights. I thought about the irresistible slope where [we] are running, who knows, perhaps toward despotism, perhaps also toward the republic, but definitely toward democracy. There are men who see in the Revolution of 1789 a pure accident and who, like the traveler in the fable, sit down waiting for the river to pass. Vain illusion!... More than six hundred years ago the first impulse was given. Some among us consider the present state as a beginning, others, as an end. It is neither the one nor the other; it is an incident in an immense revolution that began before it and has continued since."[51]

Tocqueville realized by the mid-1830s that the revolution in France had not ended, but after 1848 his conviction about the ongoing and perhaps never-ending upheaval hardened. In his *Recollections*, he observed: "The constitutional monarchy succeeded the Ancien Régime. The Republic succeeded the monarchy. The Empire succeeded the Republic. The Restoration succeeded the Empire. Then came the July Monarchy. After each of these successive transformations, people said that the French Revolution ... was over. They said it and believed it. Alas! I had myself hoped it was true during the Restoration and again after the government of the Restoration fell. And now the French Revolution has begun anew [in 1848], for it remains the same revolution as before. The farther we go, the more obscure its end becomes."[52]

In another passage, he focused on the July Revolution, but came to the same conclusion. "When viewed in perspective and as a whole, our history from 1789 to 1830 struck me as a pitched battle that raged for forty-one years between the Ancien Régime ... and the new France, led by the middle class. Eighteen thirty, it seemed to me, ended this first period of our revolutions, or, rather, our revolution, for there was only one – it was always the same, this revolution whose beginnings our parents witnessed and whose end in all likelihood we will not live to see."[53]

Unfortunately, France found itself in a long and painful period of transition, caught between the old "aristocratic and monarchical system" and the emerging "democratic and republican system."[54] "From that," Tocqueville wrote as early as 1835, "results the strange confusion that we are forced to witness."[55] Why, he wondered, did France in the nineteenth century find itself so tormented and unstable? Tocqueville's drive to understand the causes, course, and consequences of the French Revolution arose in part from his search for an answer to that question. *The Old Regime* stood as the first volume of what he planned as an extended, but ultimately unfinished, effort to solve this quandary. To a degree, the concept of a period of transition provided Tocqueville with a useful theoretical tool, a third intermediary social state between aristocracy and democracy, which helped to explain his country's predicament.

Tocqueville identified the primary cause of the French malaise as a persistent revolutionary spirit. In drafts of the 1835 *Democracy*, he denounced revolutionaries who, to achieve their ends, attacked all rights and promoted violence.[56] By 1840, he gave this destructive attitude a name. "There are certain habits, certain ideas, certain vices that belong to the state of revolution, and that a long revolution cannot fail to engender and to generalize.... Since the ordinary notions of equity and morality no longer suffice to explain and justify all the novelties to which the revolution gives birth each day, you latch onto the principle of social utility, you create the dogma of political necessity; and you become readily accustomed to sacrificing particular interests without scruples and to trampling individual rights underfoot, in order to attain more promptly the general goal that you propose. These habits and these ideas...I will call revolutionary."[57]

In a discarded fragment, he sketched a devastating "[d]efinition of revolutionary spirit. Taste for rapid changes. Use of violence to bring them about. Tyrannical spirit. Contempt for forms. Contempt for acquired rights. Indifference about the means in view of the end; doctrine of the useful. Satisfaction given to brutal appetites. The revolutionary spirit which everywhere is the greatest enemy of liberty and is such above all among democratic peoples, because there is a natural and secret bond between it and democracy.... A revolution can sometimes be just and necessary; it can establish liberty, but the revolutionary spirit is always detestable and can never lead to anything except to tyranny."[58]

Tocqueville's *Recollections* would expose the same horrible revolutionary habits and ideas among the leading actors of 1848. And one purpose of *The Old Regime* was to show the full nature of the French Revolution, both good and bad. If the Revolution had seen a glorious beginning, a shining moment when equality and liberty were combined, it had soon degenerated into violence and cruelty. The revolutionary spirit took root. "The French Revolution," Tocqueville declared in a draft, "has left in the world a spirit of uneasiness and anarchy.... This love of change for itself, this contempt for justice and for acquired rights, this attraction to tyranny and this simultaneous disgust at and horror for rules and authority,... all these things are symptoms of the same illness. This sickness is the revolutionary disease proper, a disease endemic to countries which are in revolution or have just been.... If this disease of the human mind seems more terrible this time,... this comes from the fact that the French Revolution has been the most violent, the deepest, the most fertile in catastrophes and reversals, and above all the most general revolution that there has ever been."[59]

In notes for *The Old Regime*, Tocqueville's descriptions became even more emotionally charged, and he once again linked revolutionary excesses to democracy. "As the Revolution developed; as its terrible and almost satanic character manifested itself internally; as the wild, strange, and monstrous boldness of its principles and its examples appeared; as its efforts seemed to be directed against God himself; as it overflowed its borders like a new Islam, with new ideas, new means, new tactics, knocking down, breaking, trampling over peoples and at the same time winning them to its cause; as these things burst out, people's perspectives changed. The Revolution appeared to be a fact so extraordinary, so inexplicable, that it was super-human. Some saw in it the direct action of Hell; others found in it the dissolution of society; everyone recognized an unknown future for humanity in it, something monstrous that could no longer be stopped. A feeling of horror. A sort of religious terror.... How to explain the almost unparalleled degree of violence in the Revolution? Democratic revolutions are always more violent than others.... [But] there are very complicated causes of this phenomenon which must be sought out and analyzed...."[60]

Tocqueville recognized a paradox, however. If democracy could foster the revolutionary spirit and make revolution more dangerous, it also made *great* revolutions more rare. A certain inescapable movement, uncertainty, and instability marked democratic societies. A kind of lesser or milder revolutionary agitation occurred constantly. But profound revolutions were another matter. In a draft for the 1840 *Democracy*, Tocqueville reminded himself: "I cannot say, without giving the lie to a thousand passages of this book and of the one that precedes it, that the natural tendency of equality is to make men *immobile*. Nor is that true. Equality leads man to continual *small changes* and pushes him away from *great revolutions*; there is the truth."[61]

In the text of his chapter on the topic he presented the reasons. A broad middle class; an extensive middling level of well-being; widespread property ownership; the twin desires to preserve wealth and to gain more; industrial and commercial habits and attitudes that privileged order; and entrenched public opinions, beliefs, and principles characterized modern democratic societies. All of these features favored stability and predictability and discouraged radical social, economic, or intellectual shifts.[62]

These excerpts from Tocqueville's writings touch upon the complex interconnections among equality, democracy, liberty, and revolution. Pent-up desires for equality and liberty can produce revolution: witness France. Yet equality, once established, can discourage dramatic change; and revolution can sometimes establish liberty. But as Tocqueville explained in both *Democracy in America* and *The Old Regime*, nations can grow tired of lasting disorder and instability and move toward order at any price. At that moment, ongoing revolution puts liberty at risk and opens the door to despotism.[63] Democracy can make the revolutionary spirit more destructive, but revolutionary passions can, in turn, corrupt and deform democracy, encouraging its faults and obscuring its benefits.

First-hand experience, as well as acquired knowledge of many revolutions, framed Tocqueville's analysis, informed his judgments, and conditioned his emotions. He examined both the long democratic revolution and the more specific French Revolution, devoting a major book to each. He saw 1789 through the lens of the subsequent ongoing upheavals in France, and tried, in reverse, to understand the successive revolutions in France since the 1790s by setting them against the events of the great Revolution. He enriched his study by comparing and contrasting the French experience with the American (relative) lack of revolution and the English Glorious Revolution of 1688.[64] He was particularly intrigued by the way in which England had avoided a democratic revolution in the nineteenth century; for him, the "absent revolution" said much about the weaknesses of the old regime in France. Especially after 1848, his denunciations of what he called the revolutionary spirit grew more intense and bitter. Tocqueville's fascination with revolution paralleled the draw of democracy; the two exerted a lifelong attraction on him. And behind his consideration and reconsideration of the duo remained, as always, the same concern: the future of liberty.

Concluding Comments

As the story of Tocqueville's thinking has unfolded, we have seen him, over nearly three decades, revisiting the key concepts of equality, democracy, liberty, and revolution. We have uncovered many of his most persistent concerns and ideas, elements of the subtexts that run throughout his writings, such as the tension between equality and liberty, the importance of the practice of liberty, and the tendency of democracy to threaten liberty and favor despotism. We have come upon a few characteristic analytical tools – ideal types and period of transition – and mental habits – recurring use of comparison and attempts at definition. And we have seen some examples of significant intellectual and emotional changes, including Tocqueville's attention to what he called a new "social and political morality" and his growing anger about the spirit of revolution.

A few of Tocqueville's essential purposes have been highlighted, especially his steadfast effort to explain the advantages and disadvantages of democracy and to suggest how to gain the former and avoid the latter. His proposed solutions to democratic dilemmas, we have noticed, often reflected his preference for moderation and gradualism and his desire, as a self-described "liberal of a new kind," to blend the spirit of religion and the spirit of liberty. Finally, in the course of our exploration, we have encountered Tocqueville's unrelenting critique of his contemporary French social and political world, in general, and of Napoleon, the July Monarchy, and Louis-Napoleon, in particular. Finding a path to stability, prosperity, and freedom for France and for all democratic societies remained his constant goal.

4

Consequences of Democracy: How Does Democracy Change Society?

Tocqueville's purposes were many. As he drafted his books, he habitually reminded himself in marginal jottings of his deepest convictions, larger goals, and writing strategies. In papers for the last chapter of the 1840 *Democracy*, he remarked: "I said when beginning [1835] that the march of equality was irresistible. I believe it more and more."[1] He also decided on the thematic focus for his conclusion: "Finish the book by a great chapter that tries to summarize all the democratic subject and to draw from it oratorically the consequences for the world and in particular for Europe and us [the French]."[2] What consequences, both good and bad, did democracy bring? Tocqueville, in his works, presented an array of possible results, some harmful or beneficial; others, psychological; and a few, imagined by critics of democracy. This chapter will briefly, sometimes telegraphically, review a selection of the most important of these consequences.

Harmful Consequences

Taste for Material Well-Being

According to Tocqueville, materialism, or the desire for material well-being, characterized all democratic societies.[3] Democracy, as equality of conditions, presumed a general level of comfort and widespread physical well-being. At the same time, it eroded established rankings and undermined classes, castes, families, and other traditional groupings, opening the way to greater social and economic mobility.

So democracy meant a society marked by rough equality, few fixed categories, movement, and uncertain status.

Given these features, the desire for material well-being became universal. People wanted "to satisfy the slightest needs of the body and to provide for the smallest conveniences of life."[4] They were driven to acquire, to increase, and then to preserve wealth. The goals were not only a higher standard of living and material security, but also the assertion of status. "In a democratic society," Tocqueville observed in a discarded draft of the 1840 *Democracy*, "the only *visible* advantage that you can enjoy over your fellows is wealth."[5] In the absence of traditional distinctions, money became the measure of rank.[6]

Tocqueville had perhaps first encountered such attitudes during his travels in the New World, where he found the Americans relentlessly materialistic; he saw the same desires again, however, in England in 1833 and 1835.[7] In the first volume of *Democracy*, he described the drive for well-being and wealth as primarily American; but by 1840, it had become fundamentally a democratic trait. Tocqueville also knew from his travels in both the United States and England that democratic materialism, potentially extreme, could be moderated. In the 1840 *Democracy*, he cited religion, morality, modest material ambitions, and a devotion to participation in public life as restraints on any excessive American passion for physical well-being. Religion, he realized, limited the love of wealth within the middle classes of England as well.[8]

Such forces for moderation failed to work in nineteenth-century France, however. "The passion for material well-being," he observed in notes for *The Old Regime*, "and the need to obtain it at any price was much less widespread under the old regime. There were passions close to it, but of another type,...but that quiet and tenacious passion for material well-being that we know,...which depraves less, enervates more, brings less disorder and more baseness, and which more surely than any other passion delivers men into the power of any sort of government which does not disturb their peace, and assures the success of their little business,...this taste for ease, for the conveniences of life, the idea of increasing one's fortune and employing all one's heart in this, was more rare."[9]

The desire for comfort, gain, and stability – one of the consequences of democracy – had spread throughout French society. It brought a focus on private ease, the abandonment of higher purposes and nonmaterial goals, spiritual enervation and the shrinking of souls, and a fear of any instability or uncertainty. The last trait, in particular, invited "any sort of government" that promised order. Here, perhaps, was Tocqueville's most essential fear. Focused on private well-being, people would begrudge the time and energy needed for participation in public life and prize stability above all else. "I agree without difficulty," he wrote in the 1840 *Democracy*, "that public peace is a great good, but I do not want to forget that it is through good order that all people have arrived at tyranny. ... A nation that asks of its government only the maintenance of order is already a slave at the bottom of its heart."[10] In *The Old Regime*, he told how the excesses and anarchy of the unfolding revolution had discouraged and exhausted the French and driven them into the arms of a master, Napoleon, who promised a return to order.[11] For democracy, one path to despotism was opened by the passion for material well-being.

In Tocqueville's view, democratic materialism primarily mirrored middle-class ambitions. "The passion for well-being is essentially a passion of the middle class; ... it becomes preponderant with it."[12] He did not welcome this dominance. Although he acknowledged the success of the Americans, whom he called "one part of the middle classes of England,"[13] he doubted the ability of the middle class to govern, at least in France.[14] While doing research for *The Old Regime*, Tocqueville read a 1765 report on municipal governance and concluded: "Here is the real French bourgeoisie, narrow, egoistic, and when it cannot govern solely by itself, preferring a master. What it was in 1764, it is in 1854."[15] (This time the despot was Louis-Napoleon.)

In his *Recollections*, Tocqueville portrayed the July Monarchy as the reign of the middle class, which "was definitive, and so complete that all political power, all franchises, all prerogatives, and the entire government were confined and somehow squeezed within the narrow limits of the bourgeoisie, legally excluding everything below it and in fact all that had once stood above." "The particular spirit of the middle class became," as a result, "the general spirit of the government." Tocqueville described this spirit as active, industrious, and generally orderly, on the positive side, but often dishonest, vain, selfish, timid, immoderate in the taste of well-being, and mediocre, on the negative side. The middle classes, he insisted, produced "a government without virtue and without greatness." They "made government resemble private industry ... readily forgetting the people."[16]

In 1847, in a letter to Nassau William Senior, he complained: "The system of administration that has been practiced for seventeen years [since 1830] has so perverted the middle class, ... that this class is becoming little by little ... a corrupt and vulgar aristocracy."[17] Despite having a middle-class wife and several close middle-class friends, including Eugène Stoffels and Jean-Jacques Ampère, Tocqueville's antipathy toward the bourgeoisie was unmistakable. From his perspective, the failings of the middle class largely overlapped the results of an excessive passion for material well-being.

The philosophical doctrine of materialism, which Tocqueville rejected, is not the same as the taste for material well-being. Nonetheless, Tocqueville worried that excessive attention to material needs, like the philosophy of materialism, weakened strivings toward higher, nonmaterial goals and diminished the soul. On the other hand, he believed that physical deprivation could also starve the spirit. What to do?

In discarded drafts for his chapter on religious beliefs and nonmaterial enjoyments from the 1840 *Democracy*, he wrote: "To be concerned only with satisfying the needs of the body and to forget about the soul. That is the final outcome to which materialism leads. To flee into the deserts, to inflict sufferings and privations on yourself in order to live the life of the soul. That is the final outcome of spiritualism. ... I would very much want us to be able to find between these two paths a road that would not be a route toward the one or toward the other. For if each of these two opposite roads can be suitable for some men, this middle road is the only one that can be suitable for humanity." He considered adding a small chapter where he would present an "intermediate path" and show "that in order to get men to concern themselves with the *needs* of their souls, you must not say to them to neglect the *needs* of the body, ... [and] that a certain well-being of the body is necessary for the development of the soul....."[18] Once again, Tocqueville avoided absolutes and sought a middle way. The democratic taste for material well-being, perhaps to Tocqueville distasteful even when restrained, only became dangerous when it became all-consuming.

The Reign of Commerce and Commercial Attitudes

In his 1835 travel diaries from Ireland and his drafts for the 1840 *Democracy*, Tocqueville revisited an old debate about the link between liberty and trade. Although he agreed with Montesquieu that an affinity existed between the two, he offered a gentle correction to his predecessor. "People say that the spirit of trade naturally gives men the spirit of liberty. Montesquieu asserts that somewhere. ... But I think it is above all the spirit and habits of liberty which inspire the spirit and habits of trade."[19] In *The Old Regime*, he repeated the same point, but with evidence in reverse, showing how the lack of free institutions, by discouraging such beneficial habits as working together and taking risks, hampered economic innovation in France during the seventeenth and eighteenth centuries.

In the text of the 1840 *Democracy*, he turned his major attention to the influence of democracy, rather than liberty, on economic life. He explained how democracy, by encouraging the passion for material well-being, pushes men toward commercial and industrial professions and promotes commercial and industrial activities. Democracy, he noted, turns even agriculture into a commercial enterprise.[20] Although prosperity and improvements of all sorts could result, the negative results were significant. Democracy not only led to the commercialization of all areas of society (including literature and the arts), but also created a culture of consumerism marked by the mass production of mediocre goods accessible to all. He specifically cited houses made of wood in New York that were painted to look like marble, and also the mediocre watches everyone was able to acquire. Commercial values reduced everything to the question of money and created the spectacle of people always rushing to buy and accumulate.[21]

In Tocqueville's eyes, this commercial and materialistic world, created by democracy and dominated by middle-class values, threatened liberty in particular ways. Private well-being, as we will see, threatened to become the primary goal. And although commercial habits and involvements promoted moderation and stability, they also encouraged a dangerous willingness to trade freedom, with its turmoil and uncertainty, for order, with its predictability and security. His misgivings about the democratic commercialization of society matched his distaste for the materialism of the middle class.[22]

Individualism

A third unhealthy feature characterized democratic societies: what Tocqueville labeled *individualism*. By this term, he meant neither the self-reliant, rugged individualism vaunted by Americans, nor the mildly eccentric individuality sometimes praised in England. In an outline of the 1840 *Democracy*, Tocqueville defined individualism as a harmful consequence of democracy, "a sickness peculiar to the human heart."[23] The term, relatively new in Tocqueville's time, meant for him an impulse to isolate oneself from the wider society and to withdraw into a small world of family and friends; it implied an extreme privatism that left room for private virtues, but destroyed the public virtues of civic engagement and social responsibility. Individualism dissolved broader public connections and left people indifferent to the wider society. As understood by Tocqueville, it arose largely from the desire for material well-being. It was "a considered and peaceful sentiment," that saw efforts devoted to fellow citizens and public affairs as distractions from the pursuit of private comfort and security.

Repeating in 1856 much the same language he had used in 1835 and 1840, Tocqueville defined individualism in *The Old Regime*, linking it to the "passion for material well-being, ... [which] easily mingles and so to speak interlaces with several private virtues, the love of one's family, good morals, respect for religious beliefs, ... which allows honesty and forbids heroism, and excels at making well-behaved men and slack citizens."[24] In *The Old Regime*, however, Tocqueville moved beyond what he had described in 1840, and introduced the new concept of *collective individualism*. "Our ancestors lacked the word 'individualism,' which we have created for our own use, because in their era there were, in fact, no individuals who did not belong to a group and who could consider themselves absolutely alone; but each one of the thousand little groups of which French society was composed thought only of itself. This was, if one can use the word thus, a kind of collective individualism, which prepared people for the real individualism with which we are familiar."[25] Collective individualism stood as a way station toward individualism, a dangerous step toward the complete disintegration of social bonds and abandonment of public responsibility.

During the 1840s and 1850s, Tocqueville began to pay greater attention to all the groups that composed French society and to class divisions more broadly. The topic had not escaped him either in the United States, where he had recognized the rich, the middle class, the poor, and the urban laboring classes, as well as African Americans, both slave and free; or in England, where he had described the aristocracy, the middle class, and the people (or lower classes), in general, and had noted, in particular, the grim circumstances of the factory workers in Manchester and Birmingham; or in Ireland, where he had witnessed the gap between landlords and farmers. The subject of class divisions appeared in the 1840 volume of *Democracy*, especially in the chapter entitled "How Aristocracy Could Emerge from Industry," where he portrayed the potential brutalization of the industrial working class.[26] And in his *Recollections*, reflecting on the events of 1848, Tocqueville lamented the "rancor," the "jealousies," and other passions that "would later ... stir up class warfare."[27] After his third journey to England in 1857, he contrasted, for Francisque de Corcelle, the willingness of the various classes in England to work together (despite some lingering hostility) with the attitudes in France, where "class hatreds and jealousies ... , after having been the source of all our miseries, have destroyed our liberty."[28]

Addressing this theme in *The Old Regime*, Tocqueville noted how classes had been divided and kept apart by the kings of France. "During the whole course of the long history of the French monarchy, ... there is not a single [ruler] who makes an effort to bring the classes together and unite them in any way but in submission to an equal dependence. ... The division of classes was the crime of the old monarchy." The harmful results of this collective individualism persisted. "It was no small thing to bring together again fellow citizens who had lived like this for centuries, as strangers or enemies, and to teach them how to conduct their affairs in common. It was much easier to divide them than it was to reunite them later on. We furnished a memorable example of this to the world. When, sixty years ago [in the early years of the French Revolution], the different classes which made up the society of old France reentered into contact with one another, after having been isolated for so long by so many barriers, they at first only rubbed each other's raw spots, and made contact only in order to tear each other apart. Even today [in 1856] their jealousies and their hatreds survive them."[29]

So *The Old Regime* may be read, in part, as a study of Tocqueville's concept of collective individualism, of the extreme class divisions that helped to explain the causes and course of the French Revolution. After discussing the gaps between the French nobility, the bourgeoisie, and the peasants, Tocqueville wrote: "Let us stop here before passing on, and ponder for a moment, through all these little facts that I have just described, one of the greatest of God's laws in the conduct of societies."[30] Dividing and isolating groups, causing collective individualism, could eventually turn society into a kind of dust, leaving an undifferentiated mass of similar, but detached and weak, individuals; rendering absolute government easier, but destroying any substantive centers of support; and making a sudden collapse of the entire social and political structure possible.

In the Preface to *The Old Regime*, Tocqueville presented a summary of the dangers posed by individualism and materialism. In a few paragraphs, he offered a portrait of democratic societies marked by: the destruction of aristocracy and the lack of any ties of caste, class, guild, or family among the people (a kind of social atomization); a preoccupation with private interests and the smothering of public virtues (individualism); the loss of "all common feeling, all common needs, all need for communication, all occasion for common action" (social and political isolation); a society of "astonishing mobility," where "nothing is fixed"; the inordinate desire for material pleasure and personal enrichment, love of profit, and the measure of money as "the chief means by which to distinguish between people" (the passion for material well-being); a social psychology of anxiety about status and fear about any disorder; the degradation of the human spirit and soul because of pettiness and loss of any drive toward higher purposes; and a vulnerability to absolute government or despotism.[31]

Such a picture differed in a few significant and darker ways from Tocqueville's earlier portraits of democratic society in the American republic. But as he had made clear in the 1840 *Democracy*, the United States, because of its particular circumstances, laws, and mores, had a better chance to escape individualism, extreme materialism, the collapse of common feelings and actions, the erosion of public virtues, and the coming of democratic despotism. What Tocqueville had more directly in mind as he sketched this view in *The Old Regime* was the social and political world of France since the Revolution and especially during the July Monarchy and the Second Empire. His bleak description applied unfortunately to his own countrymen.

Given Tocqueville's condemnation of individualism, it is important to remember his support for individual independence. To confuse the two would be another error. "In our times," he wrote in a draft for the second volume of *Democracy in America*, "those who fear an excess of individualism are right, and those who fear the extreme dependence of the individual are also right. Idea to express somewhere *necessarily*." In yet another variant, he elaborated: "To sustain the individual in the face of whatever social power, to conserve something for his independence, his force, his originality; such must be the constant effort of all the friends of humanity in democratic times. Just as in democratic times it is necessary to elevate society and lower the individual."[32]

Tocqueville was not speaking in riddles. In a letter to Henry Reeve in 1840, he clarified both his thinking and his fundamental purposes as a theorist. "You can be certain that the great danger of democratic ages is the destruction or excessive weakening of *the parts* of society against the *whole*. Everything that nowadays strengthens the idea of the individual is healthy. Everything that gives the species a life of its own and aggrandizes the concept of the genre is dangerous. Our contemporaries are naturally inclined to go in that direction. The realists' doctrine, when used in politics, leads to all the abuses of democracy. It facilitates despotism, centralization, contempt for particular rights, the doctrine of necessity. It favors all the institutions and all the doctrines that make it possible for society to crush people; that turn the nation into everything, and the citizens into nothing. This is one of my *central* opinions; many of my ideas converge towards it. I have reached complete conviction on this point, and the main object of my book has been to convey this conviction to the reader."[33] Paradoxically, individualism left the individual not strengthened, but weak and alone, facing the entire force of society as a whole.

Tyranny of the Majority

Among the harmful consequences of democracy pointed out by Tocqueville, tyranny of the majority is one of the best known. In his 1835 work, he reminded readers that political democracy, in essence, meant the rule of the majority, and explained how the Americans, in their state constitutions, had augmented this natural dominance and made the majority irresistible. "In the United States the majority has an immense power in fact and a power of opinion almost as great."[34]

This unchecked authority easily shaded into despotism. "Omnipotence in itself seems to me something bad and dangerous. Its exercise seems to me beyond the power of man, whoever he may be; and I see only God who can, without danger, be all powerful, because his wisdom and his justice are always equal to his power. So there is no authority on earth so respectable in itself, or vested with a right so sacred, that I would want to allow it to act without control or to dominate without obstacles. So when I see the right and the ability to do everything granted to whatever power, whether called people or king, democracy or aristocracy, whether exercised in a monarchy or a republic, I say: the seed of tyranny is there and I try to go and live under other laws."[35]

Out of this omnipotence of the majority emerged the threat not only of majoritarian tyranny, but also of legislative despotism. In the 1835 *Democracy*, Tocqueville asserted, "Of all political powers, the legislature is the one that most willingly obeys the majority," and declared: "Two principal dangers menace the existence of democracies: the complete subservience of the legislative power to the will of the electoral body, [and] the concentration, in the legislative power, of all the other powers of government."[36] Perhaps he had specifically in mind the excesses of the National Convention and the Terror during the French Revolution, democratic perversions he would address again in 1856.

Tocqueville issued two caveats about his theory of tyranny of the majority in America: first, that such abuse of power was more potential than actual, and not frequently practiced; and, second, that it threatened not on the national level, but on the state level, a qualification often overlooked, especially by his American readers. In the United States, federalism, administrative decentralization, the role of lawyers and judges, and the institution of the jury served as checks upon majoritarian excesses. More generally, Tocqueville cited humanity, justice, and reason as universal limitations on the power of the majority.[37]

Despite such safeguards, Tocqueville offered several examples of the direct physical and legal intimidation of individuals and minorities by the majority in America.[38] He argued, as well, that in the United States the majority exercised a disturbing authority over thought and opinion. "I know of no country where, in general, there reigns less independence of mind and true freedom of discussion than in America." Pointing to the impossibility of publishing anti-religious or licentious books in the United States and what he described as the "perpetual self-adoration" of the New World republicans, Tocqueville asserted bluntly: "There is no freedom of the mind in America."[39]

He developed these themes of the loss of freedom of thought and of majoritarian control over opinion in the chapter entitled, "Of the Principal Sources of Beliefs among Democratic Peoples," from the 1840 *Democracy*. As elsewhere in this second volume of his work, Tocqueville's attention had shifted from America to democracy in general. Human beings needed at least some received beliefs and opinions, he argued, and in democratic societies the judgment of the public or the mass exerted "a kind of immense pressure of the mind of all on the intelligence of each" and became one of the principal sources of those necessary accepted attitudes. The weight of common opinion increasingly shaped the thoughts and notions of everyone. The 1835 tyranny of the majority had changed into the 1840 intellectual authority of public opinion. For Tocqueville, both seriously endangered "liberty of the mind."[40]

He continued to explore the power of common attitudes as he planned and wrote *The Old Regime*. To George Lewis, he explained his research needs: "Since my goal is much more to paint the movement of the feelings and ideas which successively produced the events of the Revolution than to recount the events themselves, it is much less historical documents that I need than writings in which the *public mind* manifested itself at each period, newspapers, pamphlets, private letters, administrative correspondence."[41] In the 1856 text, Tocqueville repeatedly sought out the "public mind" and traced the influence of opinion, especially as shaped by the *philosophes*, on the unfolding of the Revolution.[42] For him, the intellectual sway of the crowd remained a major threat to individual liberty and freedom of thought.

Despotism of One Man

In the 1835 *Democracy*, Tocqueville worried not only about the omnipotence of the majority and legislative tyranny, but also about the despotism of a single man, especially a military tyrant. Reflecting on potential democratic dangers to liberty, he concluded: "I foresee that if we do not succeed over time in establishing among us the peaceful dominion of the greatest number, we will arrive sooner or later at the *unlimited* power of one man."[43] By 1840, Tocqueville's apprehensions had dramatically shifted focus, but he did not entirely abandon his concern about the despot, especially military. In his chapter on peace and war in democratic societies, he explained how war put liberty at risk by concentrating governmental authority and by opening the way to seizure of power by victorious generals. As examples, he cited, in his text, Sulla and Caesar, and, in his drafts, Bonaparte.[44] In his papers, his fears sometimes became intense. "What will the first tyrant who is coming be called? I do not know, but he is approaching. ... What more is needed for this sublime authority, for this visible providence that we have established among us to be able to trample underfoot the most holy laws, do violence as it pleases to our hearts and walk over our heads? War. Peace has prepared despotism; war establishes it. Not only as a consequence of victory, but war alone by the need for power and for concentration that it creates."[45] In his *Recollections*, he admitted, "I am by nature ... horrified by military tyranny."[46] That fear did not disappear.

In *The Old Regime*, Tocqueville retained the concept of the tyrant, especially military, not as a primary, but nonetheless as a significant potential consequence of democracy. In research notes, he reminded himself, "When I get to the Empire, analyze this fabric well: the despotism of a single man resting on a democratic base; ... the most unlimited despotism."[47] The running subtext to these enduring fears appeared to be Tocqueville's fascination with Napoleon; he longed to understand and explain Bonaparte's accomplishments and role in history. Recall that *The Old Regime* began, in Tocqueville's mind, as a book about Napoleon. His study of the *ancien régime* was a search for the point of departure behind the Revolution and the eventual rise of Napoleon. Tocqueville's assessment of the man was complex, even contradictory. He saw him as unique, a genius, "the most extraordinary being...who has appeared in the world for many centuries." But "the hero hid the despot."[48]

Whatever lasting achievements and positive characteristics were associated with Napoleon, he remained for Tocqueville the symbol of military despotism. And after the *coup d'état* in December 1851, Louis-Napoleon emerged as a pale imitation of the same democratic tyranny. "This nation," Tocqueville wrote in disgust to a fellow citizen in Normandy, "which has forgotten over the last thirty-four years what bureaucratic and military despotism is like,...is getting a taste of it once again, and this time without the seasoning of greatness and glory."[49] We see again how much Tocqueville's second great book, *The Old Regime*, was written against the background of the two Napoleons.

Centralization and the New Democratic Despotism

The link between democracy and centralization is a constant thread woven throughout Tocqueville's works, from the first volume of his *Democracy*, in 1835, to *The Old Regime*, in 1856. But over two decades, this connection assumed constantly greater importance in his thinking, and his conception of the sort of centralization most favored by democracy became radically transformed.

In 1835, he began his discussion by distinguishing between two types of centralization: *governmental*, the power to direct matters common to the entire nation, such as general laws and foreign affairs; and *administrative*, the power to direct matters relating only to certain parts of the nation and to other specific interests. He praised the first, declaring: "For my part, I cannot imagine that a nation could live or, above all, prosper without strong governmental centralization." He considered the second destructive, however, "suitable only to enervate the peoples who submit to it."[50] The story of American social and political well-being resulted, he argued, largely from the lack of administrative centralization.[51]

Tocqueville recognized that his simple distinction was imperfect. "When the same power is already vested with all the attributes of government, it is highly difficult for it not to try to get into the details of administration; and it hardly ever fails to find eventually the opportunity to do so."[52] Governmental centralization, he realized, almost always turned into administrative centralization. But the affinity of democracy for centralization remained clear. "I am convinced," Tocqueville wrote in the 1835 *Democracy*, "that there are no nations more at risk of falling under the yoke of administrative centralization than those whose social state is democratic."[53]

Tocqueville's travels to England significantly reinforced this idea. In 1833, Sir John Bowring had told him about the advantages in England of decentralization, "the chief cause of the substantial progress we have made in civilization." And a conversation with Henry Reeve in 1835 underscored the connection between democracy and centralization. After talking to Reeve, Tocqueville wrote in his travel diaries: "Centralization, a democratic instinct; ... preparation for despotism. Why is centralization dear to the habits of democracy? Great question to *delve into* in the [1840 portion] of my work, if I can fit it in. A *fundamental* question."[54]

Although Tocqueville had introduced a variety of possible despotisms in 1835, the first part of his *Democracy* often left readers with a stark choice. In the subchapter that originally ended his 1835 book, Tocqueville declared: "I feel myself led to believe that ... there will soon no longer be a place except for democratic liberty or for the tyranny of the Caesars."[55] As he drafted the 1840 *Democracy*, however, he moved away from both his flawed analysis of the two centralizations and the grim alternative he had presented earlier. In a letter to Beaumont in 1838, he described his work on the final segment of his book, "Of the Influence That Democratic Ideas and Sentiments Exercise on Political Society": "I have begun ... by establishing theoretically that the ideas and sentiments of democratic peoples make them tend naturally ... toward the concentration of all powers in the hands of the central and national authority. ... You see that I am placed very much above the point of view of administrative centralization, which consists above all of replacing secondary powers by the central power. I want to show not only that, but also the State taking hold successively of everything, putting itself on all sides in the place of the individual or putting the individual in tutelage, governing, regulating, *making uniform*, everything and everyone."[56] The true danger was far broader than he had first thought.

By 1840, Tocqueville called his 1835 vision of the unlimited power of one man "hackneyed and superficial," and declared: "A more detailed examination of the subject and five years of new meditations have not lessened my fears, but they have changed their object."[57] His habit of constant reconsideration had pushed his thinking in a different direction. Now, instead of the despotism of the Caesars,

Tocqueville foresaw a novel kind of democratic despotism; and he devoted the final fourth section of his 1840 work to his new idea.[58]

Tocqueville tried to find an original word to fit the unfamiliar concept. In a draft, he wrote: "The despotism that I fear for the generations to come has no precedent in the world and lacks a name. I will call it *administrative despotism* for lack of anything better."[59] But that term did not work. "I think that the type of oppression by which democratic peoples are threatened will resemble nothing of what preceded it in the world; ... I seek in vain myself for an expression that exactly reproduces the idea that I am forming of it and includes it; the old words of despotism and of tyranny do not work. The thing is new, so I must try to define it, since I cannot name it."[60]

In the key chapter, entitled "What Type of Despotism Democratic Nations Have to Fear," he presented the following lengthy but essential portrait of the new democratic despotism: "I want to imagine under what new features despotism could present itself to the world; I see an innumerable crowd of similar and equal men who spin around restlessly, in order to gain small and vulgar pleasures with which they fill their soul. Each one of them, withdrawn apart, is like a stranger to the destiny of all the others; his children and his particular friends form for him the entire human species; as for the remainder of his fellow citizens, he is next to them, but he does not see them; he touches them without feeling them; he exists only in himself and for himself alone, and if he still has a family, you can say that at least he no longer has a country. [A portrait of individualism, with all its faults.]

"Above those men arises an immense and tutelary power that alone takes charge of assuring their enjoyment and of looking after their fate. It is absolute, detailed, regular, far-sighted and mild. ... [It] likes the citizens to enjoy themselves, provided that they think only about enjoying themselves. It works willingly for their happiness; but it wants to be the unique agent for it and the sole arbiter; it attends to their security, provides for their needs, facilitates their pleasures, conducts their principal affairs, directs their industry, settles their estates, divides their inheritances; how can it not remove entirely from them the trouble to think and the difficulty of living? ...

"After having thus taken each individual one by one into its powerful hands, and having molded him as it pleases, the sovereign power extends its arms over the entire society; it covers the surface of society with a network of small, complicated, minute, and uniform rules, which the most original minds and the most vigorous souls cannot break through to go beyond the crowd; it does not break wills, but it softens them, bends them and directs them; it rarely forces action, but it constantly opposes your acting; it does not destroy, it prevents birth; it does not tyrannize, it hinders, it represses, it enervates, it extinguishes, it stupifies, and finally it reduces each nation to being nothing more than a flock of timid and industrious animals, of which the government is the shepherd."[61]

In *The Old Regime*, Tocqueville's denunciation of the new democratic despotism, of administrative or bureaucratic tyranny, became even more pointed. And he made the unexpected argument that such concentration of power in the state had developed during the *ancien régime* and had reached a crescendo in the middle decades of the eighteenth century with the reform ideas of the physiocrats. This group of influential eighteenth-century reformers, including Quesnay, Turgot, Le Trosne, and the elder Mirabeau, among others, favored absolute government, urged centralized control to reshape and radically transform France, and discounted any local or provincial liberty and any genuine political participation.

For Tocqueville, the old regime meant primarily the period from 1750 to the outbreak of the Revolution, a time when various significant reforms were undertaken. By 1780, he wrote, "[the] government had been transformed. Its agents were the same, but they were moved by a different spirit. As government became more detailed, more extended, it also became more uniform and more knowledgeable. It moderated itself while succeeding in taking over everything; it oppressed less while it controlled more. The first efforts of the Revolution destroyed this great royal institution; it was restored in 1800 [by Napoleon]. It was not, as has been said so many times, the principles of 1789 which triumphed then and thereafter with regard to public administration, but on the contrary those of the old regime, which were then revived and remain in existence. ... [If] centralization did not perish in the Revolution, it was because centralization itself was the beginning of that Revolution and its sign."[62] Here was one of the most original arguments of Tocqueville's 1856 book.

In another chapter, he described the fine web of control cast over French society by the state. "Under the old regime as now, there was in France no city, town, or village, no tiny hamlet, no hospital, factory, convent, or college, which could have an independent will in its own affairs, or freely administer its own goods. Then, as today, the government kept the French under its tutelage, and if the insolent word paternalism had not yet been invented, the reality had been."[63]

As noted, Tocqueville laid much of the responsibility for administrative despotism, for the omnipotent and intrusive government, at the feet of the physiocrats. "The state, according to the physiocrats, was not only to rule the nation but to shape it in a certain way; it was for the state to form the citizen's mind according to a particular model set out in advance; its duty was to fill the citizen's head with certain ideas and to furnish his heart with certain feelings that it judged necessary. In reality, there were no limits to its rights, nor bounds to what it might do; it not only reformed men, it transformed them. ... This immense social power ... , this particular form of tyranny, ... we call democratic despotism."[64]

The paternalism of the physiocrats was not the worst of it, according to Tocqueville. "We believe that the destructive theories which are known in our days under the name of *socialism* are of recent origin; this is a mistake: these theories were contemporary with the first physiocrats." He declared: "Centralization and socialism are products of the same soil. Centralization is to socialism what the cultivated fruit is to the wild one."[65] More than a trace of Tocqueville's anger, expressed in his *Recollections* and aimed at the socialist theorists, who, in his eyes, precipitated the events of 1848, reemerged in various passages of *The Old Regime*.

As we have seen, Tocqueville's 1856 work was written, in part, with Napoleon (and Louis-Napoleon) in mind. The book also served as Tocqueville's quest to understand and resolve the recurring social and political upheavals of nineteenth-century France. And it was framed, as well, by his increasingly powerful critique of the democratic despotism of the state and by his bitter denunciations of socialism. Those who read Tocqueville primarily as a critic of government paternalism or the welfare state should perhaps concentrate less on the 1840 *Democracy* than on the 1856 *Old Regime*. His argument is much more elaborate and passionate in the latter work.

Beneficial Consequences

Especially because of his portrait of the new democratic despotism, Tocqueville is perhaps better known for his descriptions of the harmful effects of democracy than for what he said about the beneficial effects. But his catalogue of the potential advantages of equality remains essential. In 1835, he devoted an entire chapter to this theme: "What Are the Real Advantages That American Society Gains from the Government of Democracy?"[66] And he made it clear that his conclusions applied not only to the New World republic, but also to democratic societies in general. He also repeatedly reminded readers in his books that democracy, without liberty, slid toward despotism. We need to underscore his conviction that, without liberty, the possible benefits of advancing equality were elusive. His chapter on the advantages of democracy highlights the following positive features.

Social Energy, Economic Activity, and Increased Well-Being

Equality of conditions, as noted, meant a more open society, without fixed ranks, and marked by social and economic mobility. Such a society, Tocqueville contended, unleashed human potential. In his chapter on democratic advantages, he first contrasted free and not-free societies, pointing out the activity and movement that distinguished the former, and noting that these features were even more applicable to democratic republics. In political life, "a sort of tumult, a confused clamor" reigned that testified to vigorous engagement in public affairs and stood in sharp contrast to the apathy and non-involvement exhibited by certain European nations (especially France) that had succumbed to materialism and individualism.[67]

In civil society, the results of democracy were as striking. Because of involvement in public affairs and interaction with others, individuals gained greater self-respect, broadened their thinking, and became more enlightened. People also developed "a general taste for enterprises" and an impulse for improvements. Tocqueville's ideas about economic matters will be examined in more detail later, but here we need to recognize his argument that democracy "spreads throughout the social body a restless activity, a superabundant force, an energy that never exists without it and that…can bring forth wonders. Those are its true advantages."[68]

Greater prosperity resulted from such social and economic activity. "[Of] all governments," Tocqueville wrote, "the government of democracy, despite its flaws, is still the most appropriate to make…society prosper."[69] Elaborating on this idea, he contrasted the potential benefits of aristocratic and democratic societies and declared that, if you want "to live in the midst of a prosperous society; if…in your view, the principal object of government is…to provide for each of the individuals that make up the society the most well-being and to avoid the most misery; then equalize conditions and constitute the government of democracy."[70]

Justice

For Tocqueville, greater justice was probably not only one of the ultimate arguments for accepting the coming of equality of conditions, but also one of the most important benefits of democracy. Justice, for Tocqueville, evoked no extreme inequality and a fluid society, with no insurmountable barriers. Given these conditions, the good things, both material and nonmaterial, of this world would be shared more equitably, among more people. And well-being of body, mind, and spirit would be more widely attainable. We will explore Tocqueville's sense of justice more fully in a later chapter, but here we can note his harsh words in the 1835 *Democracy* for the rich in England who, for their own benefit, sacrificed the good of the poor and created the greatest extremes of fortune.[71] He was signaling, as a benefit of democracy, what we would call *distributive justice.* "The real advantage of democracy ... is to serve the well-being of the greatest number."[72] And remember his declaration, cited earlier: "Equality is ... more just, and its justice makes its grandeur and its beauty."[73]

Citizenship

This beneficial consequence diametrically opposed the threat of individualism. In Tocqueville's view, democracy, understood as genuine participation in public affairs, led to citizenship. Civic engagement increased practical political experience and strengthened what Tocqueville called *public virtues*: communication and interaction with others, social awareness, a sense of common interest and shared responsibility, respect for law, sensitivity to rights, and public spirit.[74] His chapter on democratic advantages examines in turn each of these elements. And much of *The Old Regime* serves as a demonstration of the need for effective participation in government; the 1856 book illustrates what disasters may result when citizenship has been suffocated, when people have no voice, are not connected with one another, and are no longer involved in public life, and when public virtues are forgotten or abandoned.[75]

The virtues Tocqueville had in mind counteracted civic apathy and the tendency to withdraw into individualism. He also stressed how democratic participation, having and using rights, strengthened respect for rights.[76] "I wonder what way there is today to inculcate men with the idea of rights ...; and I only see a single one; it is to give all of them the peaceful exercise of certain rights."[77] He had especially in mind political and property rights. "The government of democracy makes the idea of political rights descend to the least of citizens, as the division of property [another feature of equality of conditions] puts the idea of the right of property in general within the reach of all men. That is one of its greatest merits in my view."[78]

Tocqueville candidly acknowledged the challenge of granting political rights widely, but argued that it must nonetheless be tried. "I am not saying that it is an easy thing to teach all men to use political rights; I am only saying that, when it is possible, the effects that result are great. And I add that if there is a century when such an enterprise must be attempted, that century is our own. ... There is nothing more fruitful in wonders than the art of being free; but there is nothing harder than apprenticeship in liberty."[79]

Psychological Consequences: the New Democratic Man

One of Tocqueville's strengths as a theorist comes from his sensitivity to psychology and social psychology. In his work, Tocqueville attempted to show not only how democracy would reshape society, but also how it would, to a degree, refashion human nature. For him, the coming of a new democratic social order involved the emergence of a new kind of individual, the *democratic man*. In *Democracy* and in *The Old Regime*, he included numerous summary snapshots to show how democracy transformed human perceptions, attitudes, expectations, and sentiments.[80] Some features he treated as mostly positive; others as primarily negative. But few were purely either the one or the other; if unrestrained or exaggerated, many could become destructive. As always, Tocqueville's preference went to moderation. What follows is a very brief listing of some of the more significant psychological results of democracy.

His catalogue of positive characteristics of the new democratic personality included, among other traits:

- An instinctive taste for liberty and for free institutions, and a love of independence.[81] As we have seen, however, the passion for equality could overshadow the desire for liberty, and the impulse for independence could encourage what Tocqueville called individualism.
- Milder, less harsh mores and warmer family ties. Tocqueville devoted entire chapters in the 1840 *Democracy* to these features.[82]
- Increased self-respect and greater empathy and esteem toward others. These traits also led to more benevolent or philanthropic attitudes. "There exists, in fact, among all the citizens of a democracy, ... a law for them to lend each other mutual assistance as

needed. The more similar conditions become, the more men exhibit this reciprocal disposition for mutual obligation."[83]

- A sense of similarity to other peoples.[84] Such fellow feeling could diminish national identities in favor of the "great bond of humanity." (Given the history of the last 200 years, Tocqueville may have made one of his more striking mistakes by predicting a more harmonious, peaceful world of democratic nations.) But the great dangers of feeling alike were a loss of variety, a trend toward mediocrity, and a numbing uniformity. "[Among] all these features [of the new society]," he wrote, "I seek the one that seems to me the most general and the most striking.... Nearly all the extremes become softer and are blunted; nearly all the salient points are worn away to make way for something middling.... I run my eyes over this innumerable crowd composed of similar beings.... [And] the spectacle of this universal uniformity saddens me and chills me...."[85] In *The Old Regime*, Tocqueville repeatedly denounced the physiocrats and other reformers for promoting this trend toward similarity, for ignoring the varied circumstances of a great nation, and for preferring uniform laws and regulations. Uniformity as a doctrine and as a choice became a favorite theme in his criticism of the old order.

- Steady habits and a preference for order.[86] Such inclinations, which encouraged political stability, were related to the pursuit of material well-being; but the immoderate desire for order could, of course, lead to despotism.

- An active, reforming, ambitious temperament.[87] As noted, such an attitude helped to unleash all sorts of energy, especially political and economic. Tocqueville captured some of these traits of thinking and behaving in a draft portrait. "[A man] is eager to change, the past displeases him, the present tires him, only the future seems to him to merit his thought. He scorns age and scoffs at experience. He makes, undoes, remakes his laws without ceasing. Everything changes and is modified by his indefatigable activity, even the earth that supports him. ... There are men who say that this is the American spirit and I say that it is the democratic spirit."[88]

Several of the more negative psychological results of democracy, discussed by Tocqueville, included:

- The desire for material well-being and the impulse toward individualism and apathy – what Tocqueville called the "fruit of individualism."[89] The meanings and dangers of materialism and individualism, as well as the connection between the two, have already been discussed.

- A feeling of rootlessness and isolation. Democracy dissolved traditional social bonds. The challenge for democratic society was to find new ways to nourish a sense of community and belonging.
- A sense of weakness and subservience to the crowd.[90] Here was yet another negative side of similarity and a root cause of the excessive power of public opinion and the rise of mass society.
- Arrogant trust in reason and belief in the doctrine of infinite perfectibility.[91] Although Tocqueville wanted to encourage individual independence and confidence, he called an inflated idea of human power and control "a sickness," and, in part, blamed such pride for some of the mistakes and excesses of the Revolution.
- Anxiety and restlessness.[92] Material desires constantly outpaced acquisitions. Everyone hurried to gain as much as possible, as quickly as possible. Never satisfied, *democratic man* ran out of time before acquiring all that he wanted. Despite comfort and relative well-being, a kind of chronic melancholy resulted. And anxiety about status persisted.
- Frustration, discontentment, envy, and resentment.[93] Tocqueville realized that small remaining inequalities grew paradoxically more irritating and were increasingly resented as equality advanced; and complete equality remained always beyond reach. In addition, he saw that opening the path to all meant the way was clogged with competitors and movement forward became difficult. Tocqueville also introduced the related principle of relative justice. "Men are struck much more by the inequality that exists within the interior of the same class than by the inequalities that are noticed among different classes."[94] Especially in *The Old Regime*, as we have seen, Tocqueville explained how incomplete equality and lingering privileges led to resentment and even hatred between classes. The consequences of democracy for the new democratic man, as described by Tocqueville, were emphatically not tranquility, satisfaction, and fulfillment.
- "Rising expectations." Here is another demonstration of Tocqueville's originality as a theorist. The novelty of his argument in *The Old Regime* that centralization came not from the Revolution or Napoleon but from the *ancien régime* has already been mentioned. But Tocqueville argued, as well, that the seventeenth and eighteenth centuries had witnessed increasing, if uneven, equality, that the decades preceding the Revolution were a time of growing prosperity, and that in the 1770s and 1780s the royal government

had undertaken important reforms. The events of 1789, he asserted, did not arise from rigid inequality, or entrenched economic misery, or an inflexible despotism. Instead he described a kind of "sensitivity," what we would call "rising expectations." Remaining inequalities became unbearable, economic growth increased material ambitions and made lingering miseries unacceptable, and reforms underscored the structural abuses that remained.

"I cannot insist too much ... that the very prosperity, the progress ... which in a sense made the Revolution inexplicable ..., actually explains it and ought to be considered as what announces it, as one of its chief causes. Men had become developed enough to see what they needed better and to suffer more, although the sum of their sufferings was much less than before. Their *sensitivity* has grown much faster than their relief. This is true of the grievance about freedom, and of that about equality, as well as that about money. Mine this well, because here there is not only a great perspective on the French Revolution, but an opening on the general laws that rule human societies."[95] Tocqueville's psychological insights remain remarkable. In his writings, he identified and disclosed numerous counterintuitive truths about human feelings and behavior. And notice him once again seeking out the fundamental laws that govern society.

Imagined Consequences

Faithful to his purposes and his sense of impartiality, Tocqueville presented in his writings both the advantages and disadvantages of democracy. He hoped to forewarn advocates about potential democratic failings that they overlooked and to persuade opponents that democracy offered possible benefits that they should recognize and encourage. At the same time, he hoped to dispel some charges mistakenly attributed to democracy. Parts of both *Democracy in America* and *The Old Regime* were meant to relieve the fears of critics. A few of these reassurances can be very briefly summarized.

First, democracy did not undermine religion. Tocqueville insisted that democracy and the Christian faith were compatible and offered both the Americans and the English as examples of how the *spirit of religion* and the *spirit of liberty* could be successfully blended. In both *Democracy in America* and *The Old Regime*, he attributed the anti-religious sentiments of the Revolution and its defenders not to the principle of equality, but to the overly intimate connection between the church and the old order.[96]

Second, equality of conditions did not lead to immorality and the destruction of family. In the 1840 *Democracy*, Tocqueville carefully explained how democracy tightened natural family bonds, reinforced moral behavior, allowed for traditional roles of men and women, and even produced a new concept of honor.[97]

Third, democracy did not mean anarchy and constant upheaval. Tocqueville worried, in fact, about the opposite and warned, as we have seen, against apathy, a refusal to engage in civic affairs, and a desire for order at any price.

Fourth, democracy did not mean cultural and intellectual stagnation, the end of innovation, and the loss of excellence in human society. On this matter, Tocqueville's position remained ambiguous. Even while traveling in America, he worried that equality might mean a leveling *down*, rather than a raising *up*.[98] In the 1835 *Democracy*, he chided the United States for having few notable literary or scientific figures.[99] By 1840, he carefully explained that American intellectual and cultural mediocrity came not from democracy, but from particular circumstances, especially the newness of the country and the ease with which the New World republicans could draw upon English (and European) accomplishments. The energy and activity generated by democracy, he argued, would spill over into literature, the arts, and the sciences. "Give a democratic people enlightenment and liberty," he summarized in a draft, "and you will see them…bring to the study of the sciences, letters and the arts the same feverish activity that they show in all the rest." In his text, he concluded: "So it is not true to say that men who live in democratic centuries are naturally indifferent to the sciences, letters and the arts; only it must be recognized that they cultivate them in their own way."[100]

Yet elsewhere in the 1840 *Democracy*, Tocqueville continued to wonder whether intellectual stupor was a likely consequence of democracy. In the last part of his chapter "Why Great Revolutions Will Become Rare," he shifted his attention from politics to the life of the mind and offered a powerful and eloquent portrait of democratic stagnation as alarming as his depiction of the new democratic despotism. "I cannot prevent myself from fearing that men will reach the point of regarding every new theory as a danger, every innovation as an unfortunate trouble, every social progress as a first step toward a revolution, and that they will refuse entirely to move for fear that they would be carried away. … You believe that the new societies are going to change face every day, and as for me, I fear that they will end by being too invariably fixed in the same institutions, the same prejudices, the same mores; so that humanity comes to a stop and becomes limited; that the mind eternally turns back on itself without producing new ideas; that man becomes exhausted in small solitary and sterile movements, and that, even while constantly moving, humanity no longer advances."[101] First reassurances, then warnings. On this matter, Tocqueville left his readers with a double message.

Concluding Comments

Our review of the various possible consequences of democracy has demonstrated Tocqueville's ambition and especially his originality as a theorist. He wanted to uncover the general laws that govern human society. But he especially excelled at both unexpected and counterintuitive arguments. Witness his ideas about centralization as an inheritance from the *ancien régime* and his exploration of the importance of "rising expectations."

Our survey has also shown Tocqueville searching for novel words to express his ideas. Sometimes he succeeded: *individualism* and *collective individualism*. And sometimes he failed: he found no single term to capture the concept of the new democratic despotism. As an alternative to labels, Tocqueville often resorted to summary portraits to clarify his thinking and help readers grasp his analysis. In both *Democracy in America* and *The Old Regime*, we have encountered several examples: dramatic depictions of democratic society, democratic man, the new democratic despotism, and democratic stagnation.

Finally, we have observed Tocqueville warning against extremes, such as excessive materialism, and focusing on the need for liberty. The detrimental effects of democracy, he argued, could usually be tempered by moderation. And not all the consequences of democracy named by Tocqueville would occur. Some were mutually exclusive – individualism and citizenship, for example. Others remained only latent, such as the several varieties of democratic despotism. But for minimizing the looming harmful results of democracy and encouraging the potential beneficial ones, liberty remained the essential ingredient. The consequences of democracy, good or bad, largely depended on whether democratic societies remained free. In the next chapter, we will examine some of the most important mechanisms and safeguards recommended by Tocqueville to protect liberty in democratic times.

5

Proposed Remedies: What Is To Be Done?

Near the end of *Democracy in America*, Tocqueville remarked, "The political world is changing, from now on we must seek new remedies for new evils."[1] What did he consider the best means to avoid the harmful, and encourage the beneficial democratic consequences that he foresaw? In the pages of both *Democracy in America* and *The Old Regime*, Tocqueville presented a signature package of proposed remedies that remained largely unchanged from 1835 to 1856.

In the penultimate chapter of the 1840 *Democracy*, Tocqueville identified the fundamental task as "making liberty emerge from within the democratic society in which God makes us live,"[2] and summarized the lessons that he had presented to his readers in the two halves of his book. Among suggested responses to democratic challenges, he listed: independent secondary bodies, including localities, provinces, and associations; individual rights, which evoked the specific political and civil liberties we have already examined, such as the rights to vote, speak, write, associate, assemble, and hold private property; a respect for forms and established procedures; elected, rather than hereditary, officials; an independent judiciary; and freedom of the press. In other places in both the 1835 and the 1840 volume, he also recommended deliberative assemblies, bicameralism, trial by jury, and separation of church and state. Sometimes Tocqueville simply referred to these proposals, which were primarily legal and structural mechanisms, as "free institutions." He presented as well three other important remedies related more closely to mores than to laws: the doctrine of interest well understood, the influence of religion, and the need for higher purposes; each one of this trio encouraged various habits of liberty that were essential to free democratic societies.

Tocqueville's entire catalogue of suggestions cannot be examined in detail in a brief, introductory volume. Instead, we will focus on a few of the elements that seem most important in his thinking and writing: secondary bodies, individual rights, freedom of the press, the doctrine of interest well understood, the role of religion, and the need for higher purposes.

Secondary Bodies: Localities, Provinces, and Associations

In the 1835 *Democracy*, Tocqueville gave high praise to the New England town, as a model for the local independence that "constitutes the principle and life of American liberty."[3] For him, the largely self-governing locality, which he examined in great detail, exemplified the scattering of power in the United States. He explained how the town, where the inhabitants were intimately involved in public life, produced a variety of significant moral and political effects, including town or civic spirit, training in the art of liberty, and broad practical experience in public affairs.[4]

Near the end of his discussion of towns, Tocqueville abruptly shifted his argument from localities to provincial institutions. "I believe provincial institutions useful to all peoples; but none seems to me to have a more real need for these institutions than the one whose social state is democratic."[5] Citing what he had learned in America and England from men of very different political views, he declared: "I did not meet a single one who did not view provincial liberty as a great good. ... Only peoples who have only a few or no provincial institutions deny their utility; that is, only those who do not know the thing at all, speak ill of it."[6] The message for his French audience was clear; if liberty was to be preserved in an increasingly democratic future, greater freedom for both *communes* (towns) and provinces was in order. After the February Revolution in 1848, Tocqueville, as a member of the committee charged with drafting a new constitution, remained faithful to these views and strongly supported the idea of more independence for the *communes*. Local liberties would counteract administrative centralization, providing citizens with "the intelligence to govern themselves" and allowing them to "practice governing themselves."[7] Local freedoms would, in short, provide people with training in self-government and practical political education.

In *The Old Regime*, Tocqueville wrote again of towns and provinces. He lamented the demise in the eighteenth-century French *communes* of any interest in community affairs: "The people...lived at home as if they were in a foreign country."[8] By 1750, he asserted, "[l]ocal freedoms were disappearing more and more. Everywhere the vital signs of independent life ceased; the different characteristic traits of the provinces were mixed together; the last traces of former public life were erased."[9] Without local freedoms, in either towns or provinces, people in France no longer found occasions to stay in touch or to collaborate with one another; as already noted, isolation and collective individualism were the corrosive results.

In an important appendix to *The Old Regime*, Tocqueville focused, as previously noted, on the example of Languedoc on the eve of the Revolution, where "real provincial liberty still existed." Languedoc showed readers "what provincial freedom could be under the old regime."[10] Tocqueville described the distinguishing characteristics of the province, including a well-informed and effective assembly, and a variety of vital secondary bodies – towns, villages, and administrative districts. In Languedoc, he noted, people from the various classes mingled and took part in government together.

Unfortunately, Languedoc was the exception, not the rule. "I have shown in what way the royal government, having abolished provincial freedoms, and substituted itself in three-quarters of France for all the local authorities, had attracted all affairs to itself, the smallest and the greatest alike;...France [was] the European country where political life had been longest and most completely extinct...."[11] Much of *The Old Regime* was a call for the revival of the local and provincial liberties that Tocqueville had praised in *Democracy*. He hoped to correct the long French tradition of excessive centralization, a consolidation of power that threatened to bring about a number of possible democratic despotisms.

Among the secondary bodies essential for decentralization, Tocqueville included civil and political associations. During his journey to the New World, the number and variety of associations in America had fascinated him. In 1835 he began his treatment by discussing political parties and listing towns, cities, and counties as permanent associations. He then focused on political associations, the impromptu, temporary organizations created by individuals and groups to further particular political viewpoints and causes. He also explored the ways in which the liberties to associate and assemble, freedom of the press, and the right to vote were linked. The right to associate, he noted, assumed the liberty to assemble and freedom of spoken and written expression; and wide suffrage diminished the dangers of secret, disruptive, or even revolutionary associations.[12]

In the 1840 *Democracy*, he shifted his attention to civil associations and presented a more complete theory of the science or art of association.[13] In aristocratic societies, powerful and prominent figures had assumed a natural leadership role; but in democracies, where traditional bonds were dissolved, individuals became isolated and weak. The government or the social power was left to take increasing charge of public affairs. What to do? "Possibility," he wrote in a draft, "of creating within a democratic people *aristocratic persons*, means of uniting in part the advantages of the two systems. What I mean by aristocratic persons are permanent and legal associations such as cities, *cantons*, departments, or voluntary and temporary associations.... This would have one part of the advantages of aristocracy properly speaking without its disadvantages. That would not establish permanent inequality and ... injustices.... It would create powerful individuals capable of great efforts, of vast projects, of firm resistance; it would bind men together in another way, but as tightly as aristocracy."[14]

So associations, for Tocqueville, provided an artificial, but essential, substitute for missing *aristocratic persons*, standing as rallying points for people with shared ideas, projects and goals, and serving as centers of countervailing power to the tug of centralized authority. "A political, industrial, commercial, or even scientific and literary association is an enlightened and powerful citizen whom you cannot bend at will or oppress in the shadow, and who, by defending its particular rights against the demands of power, saves common liberties."[15] Whether political, moral, intellectual, religious, commercial, industrial, general or particular, large or small, associations also taught the science of uniting with fellow citizens in pursuit of common purposes. And by stimulating "the reciprocal action of men on each other,"[16] such groupings nurtured the human heart and mind. Tocqueville did not overlook the moral results of the art of association.

Tocqueville continued in the 1840 *Democracy* to explore the connections between political and civil associations. Despite what he had witnessed in the New World, he refused to endorse an unlimited or absolute right to associate in political matters. It is important to recognize that, for him, not all associations were beneficial; for France and most other nations, Tocqueville feared political groupings that might be clandestine or violent. But political associations, he stressed, had the significant advantage of facilitating civil associations. "So political associations can be considered as great free schools, where all citizens come to learn the general theory of associations. ... When you allow [citizens] to associate freely in everything, they end up seeing in association the universal and, so to speak, unique means that men can use to attain the various ends that they propose. Each new need immediately awakens the idea of association. The art of association then becomes ... the mother science."[17] Tocqueville considered the impulse to associate as a major cause of the energy, activity, and prosperity that the American republic enjoyed.

In *The Old Regime*, civil and political associations were included among the free institutions so starkly missing in France in the decades before the Revolution. Tocqueville lamented the absence of provincial freedoms, local liberties, "living political bodies," and "organized political parties," of all the secondary bodies or organized forces that could counterbalance the central government. "When the Revolution happened," he concluded, "one would have searched most of France in vain for ten men who had the habit of acting in common in an orderly way, and taking care of their own defense themselves; only the central power was supposed to take care of it, so that the central power ... found nothing which could stop it, or even briefly slow it down. The same cause which made the monarchy fall so easily, made everything possible after its fall."[18]

In notes, Tocqueville presented a specific example of eighteenth-century associations. He cited agricultural societies as gatherings where members "debated questions in which the different classes felt themselves interested." Common discussion about shared interests served to break down the rigid separation of classes that characterized France by 1750. "[The] rapprochement and mingling of men [was] immediately felt."[19] The social and moral effects of these French societies mirrored his predicted benefits of associational activity.

Tocqueville also included federalism among the ways to avoid the concentration of power that threatened liberty in democratic nations; in the New World republic, the individual states served as additional secondary bodies, dividing authority, and standing as barriers to potential tyranny on the national level. He considered American federalism as "an entirely new theory that must stand out as a great discovery in the political science of today."[20] As a constitutional arrangement, however, it required enormous political experience and was not easily transferable to other nations. He praised federalism, in general, as a way to blend the benefits of large and small nations.[21] But for France, he dismissed the possibility of federalism and never included it among his proposed remedies for democratic dangers. His own country, he observed, remained far too exposed to powerful military neighbors to risk any form of divided sovereignty.

Individual Rights

Among remedies for the possible harmful consequences of democracy, individual rights held a privileged place in Tocqueville's political and social theory. Like the existence of free localities and provinces, civil and political rights made participation in public life and the exercise of liberty possible. In his Introduction to the 1835 *Democracy*, Tocqueville sketched an idealized portrait of the American republic as a healthy democracy. He imagined a democratic society where power was dispersed, where "the free association of citizens would...be able to replace the individual power of the nobles," and where "each person has rights and is assured of preserving his rights."[22] Throughout the 1835 volume, Tocqueville enumerated and discussed the importance of specific individual rights: to vote, associate, assemble, speak, write, and own property. Having and using these civil and political rights developed civic spirit, respect for law, and awareness of rights, your own and those of others. "Civic spirit," he declared, "seems to me inseparable from the exercise of political rights; and I think that from now on, we will see the number of citizens in Europe increase or decrease in proportion to the extension of those rights."[23] Rights, he believed, would bring forth citizens in the place of disengaged inhabitants.

Tocqueville's instinct for moderation and gradualism emerged even here, however. In drafts, he admitted: "I am not saying that political rights must be granted as of today to the universality of citizens; I am saying the unlimited extension of rights is the end toward which you must always tend."[24] But his insistence on respect for essential civil and political rights remained clear. In 1840, he declared: "So it is above all in the democratic times in which we find ourselves that the true friends of liberty and of human grandeur must, constantly, stand up and be ready to prevent the social power from sacrificing lightly the particular rights of some individuals to the general execution of its designs. In those times no citizen is so obscure that it is not very dangerous to allow him to be oppressed, or individual rights of so little importance that you can surrender to arbitrariness with impunity."[25]

In his Preface to *The Old Regime*, Tocqueville offered an eloquent, if indirect, endorsement of the individual rights he valued so highly.

"Liberty alone can effectively combat the natural vices of [democratic] societies.... Only freedom can bring citizens out of...isolation..., can daily force them to mingle, to join together through the need to communicate with one another, persuade each other, and satisfy each other in the conduct of their common affairs.... This is what I said and thought twenty years ago. Since then nothing has happened to make me change my mind."[26] The possibility of such mutual engagement in shared interests was the ultimate benefit of individual liberties.

Elsewhere in *The Old Regime*, Tocqueville's discussion of rights became less specific. He repeatedly used such phrases as free institutions, free government, or political freedom, in each case evoking the right to broad and genuine participation in public affairs. Such involvement could have avoided the disastrous lack of practical political experience that marked the *ancien régime*, leading not only to the sway of totally artificial social and political theories, but also to the excesses of the Revolution and its aftermath. In his chapter explaining how the eighteenth-century intellectuals became the leading politicians of France, he looked successively at key social groups – men of letters, nobility, and bourgeoisie – and described how each was unable to play any direct political role and was ripe to embrace a "kind of abstract and literary politics" totally out of touch with the reality of governing a great and complex nation. "We are often astonished at seeing the strange blindness with which the upper classes of the old regime, thus aided in their own destruction; but where would they have learned otherwise? Free institutions are not less necessary to the leading citizens, to teach them their dangers, than to the humblest, to assure them their rights. For more than a century,... the last traces of public life had disappeared among us...." Lacking the habitual use of freedom, "even those who ran things" (ministers, judges, intendants) suffered from profound inexperience. Only "the play of free institutions," he declared, can teach the "great science of government."[27] Without rights and free government, no one enjoyed the opportunity to practice the art of being free.

For Tocqueville, the theorist and author of *Democracy in America*, having a vote was a political right essential for developing true citizenship. But as a political figure, Tocqueville's views on suffrage were inconsistent. In both the 1835 and 1840 volumes of *Democracy*, he advocated broad suffrage. Sovereignty of the people and republican government each presumed, he argued, what was then called universal suffrage, that is, the vote for all adult males. Furthermore, the United States demonstrated, for him, that universal suffrage was less dangerous than many of his compatriots imagined. Wide suffrage spread practical political experience, stimulated civic spirit, fostered respect for law, and reduced the risks of associations by making it difficult for any group to claim to speak for a silent majority.[28]

But in the pages of *Democracy*, Tocqueville also expressed fears of excessive democracy and distrust of unfiltered democratic rule. He seemed to prefer, at least on the state and national levels, the various American constitutional provisions for indirect election, which were designed to moderate the popular will. The growing use of mandates in the United States deeply troubled him. As another check on the potential dangers of universal voting rights, he also praised the concept of representative democracy. "Of the principle of representation. It is the principle of representation that eminently distinguishes modern republics from ancient republics. Partially known in antiquity however. ... Superiority that gives to the modern ones, practicability of the republic."[29]

We need to acknowledge as well that from 1840, until the February Revolution in 1848, Tocqueville stopped supporting the expansion of suffrage. This aberration is difficult to explain. During this period, he chose to focus instead on the issue of electoral corruption. He was also apparently concerned that demands for broader suffrage would push those in power to restrict other vital liberties, such as the right to associate and freedom of the press. Yet, during the 1840s, Tocqueville continued his unrelenting criticism of the July Monarchy for being too narrowly based on the interests of the middle class and for remaining blind to the rising expectations and increasing agitation of the industrial working class. As he recognized, the selfish and short-sighted politics of his time reflected, in part, the attitudes of the tiny segment, about 3 per cent, of adult males in France who could vote in national elections under the laws of the July regime.[30] He knew that tightly restrictive voting rights were one cause of the social and political problems facing his country.

With the February Revolution in 1848, the right to vote in France was extended to all adult males, a change applauded by Tocqueville. Two years later, however, the conservative leaders of the new republic, fearful of the urban working class and the growing appeal of socialism, reversed this measure, removing the right to vote from about one-third of the newly enfranchised. Tocqueville strongly opposed this step backward from full suffrage, calling it "almost a crime."[31] He lamented the way in which the law undermined both "the prestige of universal suffrage" and the "idea of right,"[32] and worked for the repeal (unrealized) of the law the following year, in

1851. Tocqueville's original position seemed to reemerge. For him, the right to vote remained a necessary precondition of effective participation in public life.

Freedom of the Press

If Tocqueville's stand on full suffrage changed during part of his active political career, his views on freedom of the press remained consistent. He announced his position in the 1835 *Democracy*,[33] where he detailed the impossibility of finding any reasonable stopping point between censorship and freedom of the press, which involved for him the publication not only of newspapers and journals, but also of books and other printed materials. He described the principle of sovereignty of the people and freedom of the press as inseparable "correlative things." Although he recognized the possible abuses of scurrilous newspapers and coarse-minded journalists, he considered the free press an essential means to circulate ideas and opinions, to draw like-minded citizens together, and to promote the associations needed to resist the concentration of power in democratic societies. "The more I contemplate the principal effects of the independence of the press, the more I am convinced that among modern peoples independence of the press is the capital and, so to speak, the constituent element of liberty."[34]

In 1843 letters published in the newspaper *Le Siècle*, Tocqueville pointedly denounced measures taken in the mid-1830s by the government to restrict some of the liberties promised by the July Revolution, especially the right of association and freedom of the press.[35] After the 1848 Revolution, he also opposed another law, enacted in June 1850, which limited press freedom, declaring that such laws attacked organs vital to liberty.[36] And in *The Old Regime*, Tocqueville specifically criticized the half-measures of constraint that had characterized the censorship efforts of the monarchy, arguing that complete freedom of the press would have been a preferable policy.[37] His support for liberty of the printed word seemed to be unwavering from 1835 to 1856.

Constitutional Committee

Another way to approach some of the legal and institutional recommendations made by Tocqueville to protect liberty in democratic societies is to review his work as a member of the Constitutional

Committee in 1848.[38] As noted, he advocated the principle of universal manhood suffrage, which he believed necessary for the legitimacy of elections in a republic. We have also already mentioned his support on the committee for greater freedom for the *communes*. That effort failed. And, reflecting his memory of the National Convention during the Revolution and lingering fears of legislative despotism, he proposed a bicameral legislature for France, explicitly citing the American example. When that suggestion was also rejected, he argued for direct popular election of the president, believing that such a procedure would assure a strong and independent executive in the face of a unicameral assembly. To avoid the possibility of electoral corruption during a re-election campaign, Tocqueville suggested as well that the chief executive be eligible for only a single term. This proposal, which was adopted, turned out to be an error fatal to the republic. After the failure in July 1851 of a proposed amendment allowing for re-election, Louis-Napoleon found himself barred from running for president for a second term and resorted to a *coup d'état*, effectively ending both the Second Republic and Tocqueville's political career. In his *Recollections*, Tocqueville complained about the caliber of men and meager achievements of the French Constitutional Committee compared to those of the American Constitutional Convention.[39] But, despite failures, his own role on the committee at least reaffirmed some of his fundamental remedies for meeting democratic challenges.

All the legal and institutional arrangements favored by Tocqueville ultimately functioned to develop the habits and attitudes of public engagement and citizenship he believed necessary in free and stable democratic societies. Three of his other important suggestions for promoting liberty in times of equality – the doctrine of interest well understood, the role of religion, and the advantages of higher purposes – touched more immediately on perspectives and beliefs. This set of proposed remedies, he argued, directly molded the behavior and values of human beings in ways essential for healthy democracies.

Interest Well Understood

During his journey to the New World, Tocqueville discovered the striking way in which Americans merged individual interest and general interest and participated willingly, even eagerly, in public life. What he saw seemed quite new. The New England town, as imagined by Tocqueville, served as the model for a society where citizens were aware of the common good and the interests of others, were accustomed to working together, and where individual and general interests were remarkably blended.[40] In the 1835 *Democracy*, he explained this unusual understanding of interest and described the commendable behavior that resulted.[41]

By 1840, Tocqueville developed this attitude into the doctrine of interest well understood, which he described as a particular social and philosophical theory universally adopted in the United States.[42] He presented the concept as a new kind of moral value, quite unlike the republican virtue of the ancient world, but appropriate to democratic times. Instead of the sacrifice of individual interest to the common good, interest well understood meant that citizens not only had a sophisticated grasp of the general interest, but also realized that their own well-being was intimately tied to the well-being of the nation as a whole. This was not simply the doctrine that each individual's pursuit of self-interest would somehow automatically further the general interest and lead to the greater good. The idea assumed an active individual who had a sense of both self-interest and the general interest and who simultaneously pursued both.

Involvement in civic life was not, therefore, a distraction from private concerns, but an essential means both to assure public success and prosperity and to further individual interests. Properly understood, particular and common interests were not in competition, but mutually beneficial and inseparable. For Tocqueville, interest well understood, by stimulating civic participation and the practice of liberty, effectively countered the twin democratic dangers of individualism and the collapse of public life.

Despite the originality of his analysis and the important role that the idea of interest well understood played in the second volume of *Democracy*, the trajectory of the concept was short. Interest well understood stands as an example of one of Tocqueville's proposed democratic remedies that largely disappeared in any specific way from his writings after 1840. Only an indirect echo of the idea survived in *The Old Regime*, where he explained how the French – excluded in the eighteenth century and in his own time from any real political role – lost all sense of the connection between private and public interest, succumbed to the democratic danger of individualism (or collective individualism), and fell into an ultimately destructive selfishness.

Religion

Tocqueville's American travel diaries and letters home in 1831 and 1832 contain numerous descriptions of religion and its importance in the New World republic. He carried much of his journey commentary directly into the pages of the 1835 *Democracy*, where he highlighted the religious aspect of the United States, calling it one of the features that first struck his eyes, recounted the Puritan origins of the distinctive American blend of the spirit of religion and the spirit of liberty, and described the direct and indirect power of religion in America.[43]

For Tocqueville, these characteristics announced several significant principles. First, despite the fears of many of his compatriots, advancing democracy did not necessarily undermine religion; as he argued in his 1835 text, the two were not naturally at odds.[44] In *The Old Regime*, he reaffirmed this view: "To believe that democratic societies are naturally hostile to religion is to commit a great mistake; nothing in Christianity, nothing even in Catholicism, is absolutely contrary to the spirit of democratic societies, and many things are very favorable."[45] Moreover, as we have already noted, Tocqueville saw Christianity as the primary source of the idea of the equality of all human beings. One of the measures of his originality as a theorist was his enduring effort to combine the spirit of religion and the spirit of liberty; he wanted to bring together men of religious faith and friends of liberty as joint partisans of democracy. He first announced this goal in the Introduction of the 1835 *Democracy*. And nearly two decades later, in 1853, he told his friend Francisque de Corcelle: "[Man's] true grandeur lies only in the harmony of the liberal sentiment and religious sentiment; ... [my] sole political passion for thirty years has been to bring about this harmony."[46]

A second lesson from the New World emerged from a key question posed by Tocqueville. Religion served powerfully in America both to support and to moderate democracy. How did religion there maintain its strength and influence? The answer, he realized, was the careful separation of church and state.[47] The anti-religious sentiments flourishing in Europe came, he observed in the 1835 *Democracy*, from the "intimate union of politics and religion. Unbelievers in Europe pursue Christians as political enemies, rather than religious adversaries.... In Europe, Christianity allowed itself to be intimately united with the powers of the earth. Today these powers are falling and Christianity is as though buried beneath their debris. It is a living thing that someone wanted to bind to the dead; cut the ties that hold it and it will rise again."[48]

He was even more blunt in 1840. "[As] for State religions, I have always thought that if sometimes they could temporarily serve the interests of political power, they always sooner or later become fatal to the Church. ... I feel so convinced of the nearly inevitable dangers that beliefs run when their interpreters mingle in public affairs, and I am so persuaded that Christianity must at all cost be maintained within the new democracies, that I would prefer to chain priests within the sanctuary than to allow them out of it."[49] The 1840 *Democracy* also presented a significant counterexample. Tocqueville severely criticized Islam precisely because the Koran, as he understood it, presented "not only religious doctrines, but also political maxims, civil and criminal laws, and scientific theories."[50] Islam moved beyond the acceptable bounds of religion and inserted itself into the sphere of politics; this feature, Tocqueville believed, made the religion of Mohammed unsuitable for free democratic societies in the modern world.

In *The Old Regime*, he presented the same message of keeping religion away from political power. In several chapters of this 1856 book, Tocqueville asked why the Revolution had attacked religion and the church with such fury. The reason, he insisted, was "not because the Church could not take its place in the new society that was being created, but because it occupied the strongest and most privileged place in the old society which was being ground into dust."[51] And in his chapter explaining "How Irreligion Was Able to Become a General and Dominant Passion among the French of the Eighteenth Century," he included, among several reasons, the way the church "had come to join itself with the political powers ... [and] was reduced to becoming the ruler's client; between the rulers and the Church there was established a kind of exchange; the rulers lent the Church their temporal power, the Church lent them its moral authority; they made its precepts obeyed, it made their will respected. A dangerous trade...."[52]

So, to maintain influence in democratic times, religion needed to stand apart from political institutions. For Tocqueville, separation of church and state meant, most essentially, no established or state religion, no political offices or formal political functions for the clergy, and no detailed social or political (or scientific) prescriptions imposed on society by organized religion. His insistence that religion stay within its proper sphere was intended, in part, to protect the church. Binding religion to temporary and sometimes ephemeral political powers left it vulnerable and open to the rise of irreligion: witness the Revolution and its aftermath. At the same time, Tocqueville's eagerness to safeguard religion arose from his conviction that religion, by promoting healthy mores, combating such dangers as materialism and individualism, and tempering democratic excesses, was vital to the preservation of liberty in modern times. "You cannot establish," he asserted in the 1835 *Democracy*, "the reign of liberty without that of mores, nor found mores without beliefs."[53] And in a draft, he declared: "When democracy comes with mores and beliefs, it leads to liberty. When it comes with moral and religious anarchy, it leads to despotism."[54]

Despite such words, Tocqueville realized that religion did not automatically favor liberty. Dissenting once again from Montesquieu, he insisted that what ultimately upheld despotic government was not fear, but religion.[55] And he complained, especially in the 1850s, that religious preaching focused too much on private virtues to the neglect of necessary public virtues, such as the mutual obligations of citizens. "There are, it seems to me," he wrote to Sophie Swetchine in 1857, "two distinct parts to morality, each of which is as important as the other in the eyes of God, but which, in our days, His ministers teach us with a very unequal ardor. The one relates to private life: these are the relative duties of people as fathers, as sons, as wives or husbands. ... The other concerns public life: these are the duties that every citizen has toward his country and the human society to which he belongs. Am I mistaken in believing that the clergy of our time is very occupied with the first portion of morality and very little occupied with the second?"[56] Tocqueville wanted religion to take up the task of promoting citizenship.

Religion remained, for him, an essential potential remedy for democratic diseases, curbing democratic omnipotence and tempering extreme social and political actions. In the 1835 *Democracy*, he wrote: "[At] the same time that the law allows the American people to do everything, religion prevents them from conceiving of everything and forbids them to dare everything. So religion, which among the Americans never directly takes part in the government of society, must be considered as the first of their political institutions."[57] More than twenty years later, recalling his experiences in the New World, he repeated much the same argument in *The Old Regime*: "I stop the first American whom I meet, whether in his country or elsewhere, and I ask him if he thinks religion is useful for the stability of law and the good order of society; he immediately responds that a civilized society, but above all a free society, cannot subsist without religion. Respect for religion, in his eyes, is the greatest guarantee of the stability of the state and the security of individuals."[58] Religion served not only as moral restraint but also as assurance of ordered liberty. At least partly, Tocqueville blamed the rise of irreligion for the extremes and brutality of the Revolution.

In Tocqueville's social and political theory, religion had several significant functions. It supported the mores – the attitudes, opinions, and behaviors – necessary for a healthy democracy; checked democratic extremism; taught moral values, including private and, ideally, public virtues; enlarged the hearts and souls of human beings by raising their vision beyond simply the material and the immediate; supplied people with authoritative answers to difficult spiritual questions; and upheld liberty. Although Tocqueville usually treated religion as a possible remedy for democratic dangers, he did not see religion solely in utilitarian terms. He believed deeply that human nature turned innately toward religion, faith, and things spiritual. For him, religion was more than the sum of its uses; it resonated with the human soul.

In a passage from the 1835 *Democracy*, Tocqueville summarized the remarkable harmony that existed between the religious and political tendencies in colonial New England. "Religion sees in civil liberty a noble exercise of the faculties of man; in the political world, a field offered by the Creator to the efforts of intelligence. Free and powerful in its sphere, satisfied with the place reserved for it, religion knows that its dominion is that much better established because it rules only by its own strength and dominates hearts without other support. Liberty sees in religion the companion of its struggles and triumphs, the cradle of its early years, the divine source of its rights. Liberty considers religion as the safeguard of mores, mores as the guarantee of laws and the pledge of its own duration."[59]

This analysis revealed in a nutshell several of Tocqueville's fundamental and enduring principles concerning religion as a democratic remedy: the need to separate the worlds of religion and politics; the seemingly contradictory goal of tying religion and civil society closely together in order to benefit from the power and influence of religion; and the role of religion as the "safeguard of mores" suitable for the preservation of liberty.

Higher Purposes

To counter the tendency toward pettiness and the fixation on small needs and narrow desires that materialism and individualism encouraged in democratic societies, Tocqueville also recommended the pursuit of higher purposes, especially patriotic enterprises. For him, national pride worked to counteract apathy, raise vision, and expand souls; patriotism stood as another possible remedy for democratic ills.

In his research notes for the incomplete portion of *The Old Regime*, Tocqueville wrote: "When we look at it from a broad and general point of view, patriotism, despite all the great actions which it has motivated, seems a false and narrow passion. It is to humanity that the great actions suggested by patriotism are due, not to that little fragment of the human race closed within their particular limits that we call a nation and a country." But he proclaimed this view wrong. "Man, as God has created him (I don't know why), becomes less devoted as the object of his affections becomes larger. His heart needs the particular; it needs to limit the object of its affections in order to grasp the object in a firm and lasting embrace. ... I am convinced that we better serve the interests of the human species in giving each man only a particular country to love than in wanting to inspire him on behalf of the human species, which, whatever we do, he will only consider with a distant, uncertain, and cold gaze."[60]

This conviction, which reflected Tocqueville's own intense nationalism, sometimes led him into contradictory positions. Although he knew, for example, that war led certainly to the centralization and possibly to the military tyranny he so feared, he nonetheless praised war as a solution to democratic blandness and loss of purpose. In the 1840 *Democracy*, he observed: "I do not want to speak ill of war; war almost always enlarges the thought of a people and elevates the heart. There are cases where it alone can arrest the excessive development of certain tendencies that arise naturally from equality, and where war must be considered as necessary for certain inveterate illnesses to which democratic societies are subject."[61]

He also ardently desired a high profile for France on the international stage, which meant support for French imperialism. The Algerian conquest and colonization, launched in 1830, captured Tocqueville's attention. In the 1830s and '40s, he wrote various articles and reports, gave speeches, and twice visited Algeria (1841 and 1846). Although he criticized the excessive violence and brutality of the French military campaigns, he favored the Algerian project, believing that France had a legitimate civilizing mission and needed to assert a French presence in North Africa. At first, he believed in the possibility of melding the French and native Algerian populations. He soon abandoned that vision, however, and promoted the idea of two separate peoples, living side by side, but in different territories. Hoping to encourage French settlers, he advocated basic liberties for the colonists, including greater local self-government, but his commitment to freedom did not extend to basic liberties for the Algerians.[62]

Such attitudes expose some of the inconsistencies in Tocqueville's thinking. He recognized war both as an engine for centralization and a breeding ground for military dictatorship, and as a tonic for democratic lassitude. As we will see, his bellicose attitude would later put him at odds with John Stuart Mill. Tocqueville also believed in empire, embraced the concept of a special mission for France, and promoted essential freedoms for one population in Algeria (the French colonists), but not for another (the various groups of native Algerians). In this case, his love of national glory seemed to outweigh his attachment to liberty. These contradictions, which he left unresolved, continue to tarnish Tocqueville's reputation among some readers and commentators.

Concluding Comments

What do Tocqueville's proposals tell us about the larger goals and underlying assumptions of his social and political theory? By advocating what he labeled *free institutions*, as well as by calling for a prominent role for religion, acceptance of the doctrine of interest well understood, and the promotion of patriotic passions, Tocqueville aimed, above all, to broaden participation in public life and to promote the practice of liberty. Just as the regular observance of religious rituals is sometimes suggested as a path to genuine faith, the habitual exercise of liberties could, in Tocqueville's eyes, lead to true freedom.

Of course, Tocqueville's suggested remedies, especially his legal and institutional proposals, also illustrate his desire to distribute power, to strengthen *secondary bodies* (especially localities, provinces, and associations) in the face of society as a whole.[63] Consolidated power, wherever it accumulated, promised a future of democratic despotism, rather than democratic freedom. Resistance to centralization remained a core purpose of Tocqueville's program for democratic liberty.

But the heart of his social and political theory lies not only in warnings about the concentration of power, but also in his insistence on developing the habits of liberty. "There is," he wrote in the 1835 *Democracy*, "nothing more fruitful in wonders than the art of being free; but there is nothing harder than apprenticeship in liberty."[64] Only the practice of liberty could teach the mores needed for freedom. Training in liberty developed citizenship and public virtues and helped to counter many of the harmful consequences of democracy. Behind Tocqueville's alarms about centralization is the theme of securing freedom by exercising suggested rights and liberties. Perhaps too often the attention of readers is caught on the issue of centralization without recognizing the crucial role of the *doing* of liberty. For Tocqueville, a healthy, stable, and free democracy required the broadest possible involvement in public affairs. Democracy, in his social and political theory, meant participatory democracy. Without the opportunity for widespread engagement in civic life, both democracy and freedom itself amounted to a sham.

Also among the principles woven throughout Tocqueville's writings is his conviction that, over time, laws can reshape mores and, at least to a degree, transform human beings. Most of the measures he suggested to safeguard liberty were essentially legal or structural tools designed to produce the attitudes, habits, values, and behaviors he considered essential for healthy democracies. The right mores could counterbalance such negative democratic moral tendencies as excessive materialism, individualism, and apathy, and could bring forth citizens who would be experienced in public affairs, attuned to rights, aware of social and political complexities, and alert to possible democratic abuses. Exercising the liberties recommended by Tocqueville would also broaden hearts and minds by putting citizens in contact with each other, forcing them to mingle, to deliberate, to learn how to combine private and public interests, and to work toward common goals. Here were many of the public virtues essential to the citizenship prized by Tocqueville. To legislators and constitution-makers fell the task of enacting laws and founding institutions that would educate and mold democratic peoples. Tocqueville's abiding interest in promoting engagement in civic life also underscored his insistence on human moral responsibility. Ultimately, as we have seen, citizens in democratic societies bore the burden of choosing whether democracy would lead to liberty or to despotism.

In our review of Tocqueville's remedies, we have once again witnessed his preference for moderation. His willingness to extend rights, especially suffrage, but not necessarily all at once or to all; his recurrent fear of excessive democracy or the unfiltered popular will; his focus on "a moderate, regulated liberty disciplined by faith, mores, and laws";[65] and his language of apprenticeship: all speak to his instinct for gradualism. We will see other examples of this characteristic when we look at some of his suggestions about social questions and other matters important during his political career.

We also need to remember that Tocqueville's proposed solutions for democratic dangers were primarily aimed at his own country. In a letter written in 1839 to Henry Reeve, who translated *Democracy in America* into English, Tocqueville explained the basic purposes of his book. "This work is, in a word, written principally for France or, if you prefer modern jargon, from the French point of view. I write in a country and for a country where the cause of equality has henceforth won, without possible return toward aristocracy. In this situation, I felt that my duty was to stress particularly the bad tendencies that equality *can* bring about in order to try to prevent my contemporaries from surrendering to them. It is the only honorable task for those who write in a country where the struggle is finished. So I say truths often very hard to the French society of today and to democratic societies in general, but I say them as a friend and not as a critic. It is even because I am a friend that I dare to say them."[66]

This purpose clearly informed the writing of *The Old Regime* as well. In the Preface to that book, Tocqueville wrote: "I do not pretend to have written [the present work] without passion. It would hardly be possible for a Frenchman to feel nothing when he speaks of his country and ponders his times. I admit that in studying our old society in all its aspects, I have never entirely lost sight of our modern society. I wanted to discover not only what illness killed the patient, but also how the patient could have been cured. I have acted like a doctor, dissecting every organ in order to discover the laws that govern the whole of life. ... I have also taken care to cast light on the vices which, having devoured the old society, continue to gnaw at our own, so that in seeing the evil they have done, we can better understand the evil they can still do."[67] So both of Tocqueville's major works were written, above all, with France in mind. He hoped to persuade his countrymen to accept and make the best of advancing democracy. He meant his books as guides on how to avoid democratic pitfalls, find good paths forward, and end up not at despotism, but at liberty.

Finally, it is important to recognize the unusual nature of the group of remedies put forth by Tocqueville. His signature cluster of solutions included blended commitments to the spirit of religion and the spirit of liberty, a preference for active liberty, and an insistence on participatory democracy. True freedom, for Tocqueville, was informed by moral restraint and realized only by dedicated engagement in public life. In a draft for the 1840 *Democracy*, he encapsulated his message: *"Use democracy to moderate democracy. That is the sole path of salvation that is open to us. Discern the sentiments, the ideas, the laws that, without being hostile to the principles of democracy, without being naturally incompatible with democracy, can however correct its unfortunate tendencies and, while modifying it, become incorporated with it. Beyond that everything is foolish and imprudent."*[68]

6

Economic Ideas and Social Reform

Not infrequently, Tocqueville is portrayed as a social and political theorist, a political philosopher, quite unaware of and minimally interested in economic matters and the social issues of his day. This perspective is a serious misreading of Tocqueville's thinking and writing. Since the 1960s, a growing number of scholars have explored his ideas about economic and social issues in modern democratic societies.[1] Two of the more recent studies pointedly praise the breadth and originality of his economic reflections and the thoroughness and pioneering nature of his research and insights on social matters.[2]

Economic Ideas

Even before his American journey, Tocqueville began to read and study political economy. Jean-Baptiste Say (1767–1832), perhaps the most important French economic theorist of his generation, had presented a series of lectures in 1828, subsequently published as *Cours complet d'économie politique pratique* [*Complete Course of Practical Political Economy*].[3] Say's work captured Tocqueville's interest. He took detailed notes on his first reading, and then carried Say's book with him across the Atlantic for continued study. With Say, Tocqueville explored the role of self-interest in political economy, the serious danger of growing poverty, the connection between economic and political liberty, the social and economic arguments favoring widely held small landholdings, and the primary economic role of industry in modern societies. Tocqueville also noted Say's critique of the physiocrats, an assessment he would reproduce, perhaps more on political than economic grounds, nearly three decades later in *The Old Regime*.

Tocqueville learned as well from the work of Nassau William Senior, the most prominent English economist in the first half of the nineteenth century.[4] Tocqueville first met Senior in 1833, during his initial brief journey to England; and the two men quickly formed an enduring friendship. Despite many letters and conversations together, however, Senior's influence on Tocqueville's economic ideas remained limited. His understanding of political economy was too narrow and abstract to appeal to Tocqueville. Senior saw the field as essentially a science and wanted to separate economics from politics. He also favored large estates rather than small landholdings. Perhaps his major impact on Tocqueville's thinking arose from the English Poor Law of 1834, which was shaped primarily by Senior. Tocqueville, echoing Say, strongly disagreed with Senior's approach to helping the poor. English legislation, Tocqueville believed, created a system of public charity that worsened the condition of the poor, forced them to remain in their parishes, and turned them into an idle and dependent class. But the law and its consequences undoubtedly stimulated Tocqueville's interest in the problem of poverty in modern societies.

The third and perhaps most influential political economist studied by Tocqueville was Alban de Villeneuve-Bargemont, author of *Economie politique chrétienne, ou Recherche sur la nature et les causes du paupérisme en France et en Europe* [*Christian Political Economy, or Research on the Nature and Causes of Pauperism in France and in Europe*] (1834).[5] Tocqueville, who knew Villeneuve-Bargemont and read his book, resonated both to his compatriot's broad approach and to his emphasis on the moral dimension of economic issues. The lasting imprint of Villeneuve-Bargemont on Tocqueville's ideas appears in four crucial areas: the causes of and possible cures for poverty; the portrayal of the new industrial aristocracy as a new and cruel feudalism; the argument for the moral obligation of individuals and society to confront growing poverty; and a roster of suggested solutions to the problem of poverty.

This trio certainly does not exhaust the list of political economists who influenced Tocqueville.[6] Here, however, our purpose is not to examine his sources, but to underscore his interest in the economic and social issues of his day and to consider some of the major currents in his economic thinking.

Tocqueville's attention to economic matters was already on display during his American journey. In the New World, contrary to the

opinion of some critics, Tocqueville grasped the physical, techno-
logical, and economic transformations then taking place in the
American republic.[7] In his travel diaries he recorded such details as
immigration statistics, population growth in cities and states, and the
cost of constructing and running steamboats, operating a sugar cane
plantation, and paying the salaries of public officials. More broadly,
in his journey notes (as well as in the 1835 *Democracy*), Tocqueville
described the general level of well-being, the widespread property
ownership, and the universal movement that characterized the United
States. Everything, even the land, seemed in motion. He witnessed
a universal drive for improvement and new opportunities, which
pushed Anglo-Americans relentlessly from profession to profession
and place to place. If he failed to visit any factory during his travels,
he did recognize the rise of manufacturing and even noted the rise
of a new type of commercial and industrial association, the corpora-
tion. The entire continent, he sensed, was being transformed both
geographically and economically.

How did the Americans manage to accomplish such wonders?
Their approach led Tocqueville to reconsider the role of government
in economic development, an issue that he would revisit repeatedly
in his later writings. "I only know of one means of increasing the
prosperity of a people, whose application is infallible," he observed in
one of his travel notebooks. "That means is none other than increasing
the facility of communication between men. On this point what can
be seen in America is both strange and instructive. ... America has
undertaken and finished the construction of some immense canals.
It already has more railways than France; no one fails to see that the
discovery of steam has incredibly increased the power and prosperity
of the Union. ... As to the means employed, ... this is what I noticed
about the matter.

"It is generally believed in Europe that the great maxim of government in America is that of laisser-faire ...; that is a mistake. The
American government does not interfere in everything, it is true,
as ours does. It makes no claim to foresee everything and carry
everything out; it gives no subsidies, does not encourage trade, and
does not patronize literature or the arts. But where great works of
public utility are concerned, it but seldom leaves them to the care
of private persons; it is the State itself that carries them out. ... But
it is important to observe that there is no rule about the matter. The
activity of companies, of [localities], and of private people is in a
thousand ways in competition with that of the State. ... So then no
exclusive system is followed; in nothing does America exemplify

a system of that uniformity that delights the superficial and meta-physical minds of our age."[8]

As we have noted, Tocqueville also recognized how democracy, in the United States, encouraged the pursuit of material well-being, spurred social and economic energy, promoted prosperity, and developed commercial attitudes and habits. As he traveled, he carefully observed the harmful economic effects of slavery, contrasting in particular the free and slave sides of the Ohio River. He also did not miss the westward movement. The rapid, almost providential expansion of the Anglo-Americans toward the Pacific astonished him, but he lamented the American greediness to seize the land and its resources and foresaw the likely results for other nations and peoples of such a continental destiny, dangerous to Mexico and probably fatal to Native Americans.

Research required by the penitentiary study, the ostensible reason for the New World journey, also made Tocqueville aware of the problems of crime and poverty in the United States. Although he would ultimately focus on equality of condition as the defining characteristic of American society, he knew about persisting inequalities of race and class. The question of poverty in particular would become one of the major themes in his social and economic thinking.

After his return from the New World, Tocqueville, we recall, briefly visited England for about five weeks in 1833. There he launched his long comparison of open and closed aristocracies, a distinction that would reappear in the pages of *The Old Regime*; witnessed in various court rooms the operation of the English system of poor relief; encountered another nation marked, like the American republic, by the power of money; deepened his consideration of social and political classes; and glimpsed, for the first time, English industrial development.

His return to England and visit to Ireland in 1835, after the publication of the first volume of *Democracy*, had even more significant and lasting effects on his social, political, and economic theories.[9] As already indicated, the English example pushed Tocqueville to analyze more fully the connections between democracy and centralization. But economic lessons were as important. His visits to Birmingham and Manchester demonstrated the stunning scale and human costs of industrialization. He was forced to examine the links between advancing industry and growing poverty and to consider the terrible living and working conditions of the new industrial working class. In his travel diaries, he described what he saw in Manchester.

"Thirty or forty factories rise on the tops of the hills.... Their six stories tower up; their huge enclosures give notice from afar of the centralization of industry. The wretched dwellings of the poor are scattered haphazard around them.... Heaps of dung, rubble from buildings, putrid, stagnant pools are found here and there among the houses.... But who could describe the interiors of these quarters set apart, home of vice and poverty, which surround the huge palaces of industry and clasp them in their hideous folds.... Narrow, twisting roads ... are lined with one-story houses whose ill-fitting planks and broken windows show them up, even from a distance, as the last refuge a man might find between poverty and death.... Below some of [these] miserable dwellings is a row of cellars to which a sunken corridor leads. Twelve to fifteen human beings are crowded pell-mell into each of these damp, repulsive holes. The fetid, muddy waters [of one of the streams], stained with a thousand colors by the factories they pass,... wander slowly round this refuge of poverty.... It is the Styx of this new Hades."[10] Tocqueville would never totally forget this horrific vision.

Ireland displayed, not new industrial, but entrenched agricultural poverty. In his Irish notebooks, Tocqueville found himself reconsidering not only the economic, but also the social and political advantages of widespread small property holdings. And the aristocracy in Ireland provided him with yet another (disturbing) aristocratic model. Once again, shocking poverty confronted Tocqueville and forced him to search for probable causes and possible cures. On July 9, 1835, he visited a Poorhouse in Dublin. "*The sight within*: the most hideous and disgusting aspect of wretchedness. A very long room full of women and children whose age or infirmity prevents them from working. On the floor the poor are seated pell-mell like pigs in the mud of their sty. It is difficult to avoid treading on a half-naked body. In the left wing, a smaller room full of old or disabled men. They sit on wooden benches, crowded close together.... They do not talk at all; they do not stir; they look at nothing; they do not appear to be thinking. They neither expect, fear, nor hope anything from life."[11] The image of such degradation and the hollowing out of the human spirit would continue to haunt Tocqueville's later thinking and writing.

Beyond lessons learned from readings and travel, what significant economic views does Tocqueville express in his major works, *Democracy in America* and *The Old Regime*? The manuscripts and text of the 1835 *Democracy* include a variety of noteworthy discussions of political economy. Most were focused on the material and economic features of America, rather than on democracy in general. But they are early statements of themes that would continue to appear in Tocqueville's later writings. In various drafts, Tocqueville touched on certain matters that he decided not to include in final versions of his 1835 work. His manuscripts, for example, contain additional discussions of tax policies and revenues, of the dangers of manufacturing districts, and of the threat to equality posed by industry, even in America.[12] Even though Tocqueville temporarily put these particular ideas aside, he did address several other significant topics in the first portion of his *Democracy*. For example, he examined the pressures on public expenditures in democratic societies, expressed his concern about the increasing number of industrial workers concentrated in large cities, and explained how modern division of labor diminished the worker.[13] Perhaps as significantly, he also explored the economics of slavery, condemning the "peculiar institution" not only as immoral, but also as inefficient and destructive to economic development. He would return to this subject in his later writings on abolition.[14]

In his chapter on the American social state, he discussed as well the importance of inheritance laws for encouraging widespread property ownership and for speeding the demise of any traditional landed quasi-aristocracy in the United States. Laws about land inheritance, he asserted, played a key role in the coming of equality of conditions. "I am astonished," he wrote, "that ancient and modern political writers have not attributed a greater influence on the course of human affairs to the laws of landed inheritance. ... Constituted in a certain way, the law of inheritance reunites, concentrates, gathers property and, soon after, power, around some head .... Driven by other principles and set along another path, its action is even more rapid; it divides, shares, disseminates property and power. Sometimes people are frightened by the rapidity of its march. ... It crushes or sends flying into pieces all that gets in its way; it constantly rises and falls on the earth until nothing is left in sight but a shifting and intangible dust on which democracy takes its seat."[15] Tocqueville's interest in inheritance laws and his preference for small landholdings would endure and reemerge in the *The Old Regime*, as well as in other essays.

Before the 1840s, Tocqueville's most extensive discussion of economic and social issues in modern democratic societies appeared in the second volume of *Democracy*. Throughout the 1840 work, he addressed an impressive variety of economic and social matters. Best known is his chapter, reflecting the influence of Villeneuve-Bargemont, entitled "How Aristocracy Could Emerge from Industry."[16] There Tocqueville presented "two new axioms of industrial science": economy of scale and division of labor. And he once again discussed the way in which industrialization leads not only to growing poverty, but also to a new kind of aristocracy that threatens democratic equality. He lamented the loss of mutual obligation or bond between the industrialist and the worker, the rich and the poor. But his central concern remained the brutalization of the laborer. "[The] man," he declared, "becomes degraded as the worker improves."[17]

Elsewhere in the 1840 *Democracy*, Tocqueville presented many other significant economic issues: the concept of inheritance laws appropriate for preventing the perpetuation of wealth in families but still allowing for the accumulation of wealth;[18] the need for supporting a fluid democratic society, for encouraging social and economic mobility; the link between democracy and the passion for material well-being; the connection between the habits of commerce and those of liberty; the boost given by democracy to the idea of work and to respect for all professions; the influence of democracy on salaries, rents, and contracts; the encouragement given in democratic society to commercial and industrial activities, turning even agriculture into a trade; and the general commercialization of society, the development of mass production and consumption, and the acceptance of planned obsolescence. We have already touched upon several of these items.

He also addressed key topics related to industrialization, including the recognition that "the progress of equality and the development of industry are the two greatest facts of our times";[19] the development of great industrial enterprises; the danger of recurring industrial crises; the need for the industrial class [(the industrialists)] "to be regulated, supervised and restrained" and for industrial associations (corporations) to be put under some control by the social power;[20] and the dangerous relationship between industrialization and the concentration of power in the state. The impulse toward centralization came not only from democracy but also from industrialization.

After the 1848 Revolution and particularly the violence of the June Days, the emphasis of Tocqueville's economic thinking shifted somewhat. In his *Recollections*, he focused especially on issues relating to property, casting the June Days as the sign of a new conflict between those with property and those without. He strongly denounced socialist theories as feeding class antagonism and undermining the right of property. Holding property, he argued, created social bonds among owners of all sorts and encouraged social harmony. He also pointed out the dangers of the growing concentration in Paris of industrial workers, the class most influenced by socialism.[21]

All these topics would reappear in *The Old Regime*. But in 1856 Tocqueville would cast a much wider net of ideas. He presented the economic policies and failings of the *ancien régime* in considerable detail, exposing the corrupt methods used to raise revenue and the profound injustice of the system of taxation. "Of all the ways to make distinctions between people and classes," he wrote, "inequality of taxation is the most pernicious."[22] Returning to a topic first explored in the 1835 *Democracy*, he also examined the effects of land inheritance laws. Tocqueville discussed as well the extensive number of small rural properties and the economic pressures facing the French peasantry as landowners. And he traced the economic and political assumptions of the physiocrats, offering, as we have noted, a scathing critique of their ideas, especially about the omnipotent role of the state. Tocqueville recognized the growing wealth of the bourgeoisie and the general prosperity in France by the mid-eighteenth century, but, as he pointed out, centralized control and misguided economic policies choked innovation and suppressed industrial development. All was not negative. He also briefly presented the economic achievements of the Revolution.[23]

Overall, Tocqueville devoted great attention in his 1856 book to the economic dimensions of France in the seventeenth and eighteenth centuries. His treatment of economic topics remains impressive. Arguably, *The Old Regime* may be read in yet another way, as a study of the political economy of the *ancien régime*. Mistaken economic policies, he asserted, help to explain the collapse of the monarchy and the coming of the Revolution.

Tocqueville always assumed the inescapable interconnections among diverse areas of society. Predictably, his approach as a theorist of political economy emphasized, above all, the broader moral dimension of economics. He did not consider political economy simply as a science divorced from mores and social institutions.[24] Economic arrangements and developments, in his view, were profoundly shaped not by abstract scientific laws, but by attitudes, behavior, ideas, and beliefs – in short, by habits of the heart and mind. In the field of political economy, he also recognized and repeatedly examined the interplay of advancing equality of conditions, economic and industrial development, the problem of poverty, and the appropriate role of the state. The links among this quartet – democracy, industrialization, poverty, government intervention – largely defined the unfolding pattern of his economic thinking and writing.

Perhaps in some ways the issue of poverty became central to Tocqueville's interest in economic matters. His readings in the 1820s and beyond, his study of prison reform in the early 1830s, and his first-hand experiences, especially in 1835, demonstrated that democracy and industry were locked together and that increasing industrialization meant growing poverty (for some). What he learned presented him with a complicated puzzle. Tocqueville found himself face to face with difficult questions about the causes of and possible remedies for poverty. The man of theory and of action took on the role of moderate social reformer.

Social Reform

On economic and social matters, the temptation to focus primarily on Tocqueville's *Democracy in America* and *The Old Regime* needs to be resisted. His other writings from the 1830s and 1840s complete the picture of Tocqueville as political economist and moderate reformer.

After the appearance of the 1835 *Democracy* and while drafting the 1840 volume, Tocqueville wrote two important essays on the topic of poverty: the first, *Memoir on Pauperism*, appeared in 1835, and the second, drafted in 1837, was left incomplete and never published. Except for the report on the American penitentiary system (1833), these two essays stand as Tocqueville's first writings on social reform. His proposals for alleviating poverty may be understood as additional suggested remedies for particular dangers facing modern democratic societies.

Memoir on Pauperism is a notably severe document, unlike most of Tocqueville's other writings on social questions. It distinguishes sharply between two kinds of welfare: private, individual charity and public or legal charity. Tocqueville used the example of the various English poor laws to show how legal charity "creates an idle and lazy class," locked in dependency and morally degraded. Public charity, or "the right of the poor to obtain society's help," he wrote, must therefore be avoided. But developing industrialization, he recognized, led not only to greater wealth and prosperity for some, but also to growing poverty for others. Individual charity alone, Tocqueville admitted, would be inadequate for alleviating the increasing problem of pauperism. He concluded his harsh portrayal of the poor and strong condemnation of government aid by asking a series of general questions that only hinted at solutions he would propose later.[25] He also conceded: "I recognize not only the utility but the necessity of public charity applied to inevitable evils such as the helplessness of infancy, the decrepitude of old age, sickness, insanity. I even admit its temporary usefulness in times of public calamities.... I even understand ... public charity which opens free schools for the children of the poor. But I am deeply convinced that any permanent, regular, administrative system whose aim will be to provide for the needs of the poor, will breed more miseries than it can cure."[26]

Tocqueville sounded a quite different tone in the 1837 essay, in which he moved beyond unresolved questions and suggested several specific measures to alleviate poverty.[27] He began the essay by describing agricultural and industrial poverty. He argued that, in France at least, the rural poor who possessed small landholdings were less vulnerable during economic downturns. The essential difficulty for the industrial working class was absolute dependency on their own labor; they owned nothing and, in times of economic crisis and the loss of employment, found themselves completely without resources.

For Tocqueville, the solution was to develop new ways to make industrial workers into holders of some kind of independent property and develop among them the spirit and habits fostered by property ownership. In his essay, he explored several possible means to achieve this end, but settled on the establishment by the government of special savings banks in combination with a reformed French system of *monts-de-piété*, or pawnshops, that offered guaranteed loans to the poor. Such a new type of savings and loan institution would allow the industrial working classes to establish small personal accounts, turning them into property holders and providing essential resources in times of need. Tocqueville did not suggest how the desperately poor industrial worker would find any extra money to save, but his treatment of the indigent was far less harsh, and he at least suggested a specific remedy for economic problems that he would offer repeatedly in the 1840s.

Another crucial reform proposal in 1839 focused not on poverty, but on slavery. Tocqueville offered his *Report on Abolition* as the inaugural presentation of a newly elected member of the Chamber of Deputies.[28] As a member of the commission charged with examining the issue of abolition in the French colonies, he summarized the conclusions of the study group. After emphasizing the recognized evil of slavery and the certainty of its eventual end, he highlighted three principles agreed upon by the committee: the radical position of immediate (rather than gradual) emancipation; an indemnity to be paid to the slaveholders; and a strict system of apprenticeship for the newly freed slaves, including education and training in the habits of liberty. This idea of apprenticeship strangely echoed Tocqueville's own concept of the practice of liberty. "It is only the experience of liberty," he wrote, " ... which can prompt and form in man the opinions, virtues, and habits which suit a citizen of a free country."[29] The French state would be the "sole guardian" of the enfranchised laborers, paying wages and overseeing their treatment. The exercise of appropriate governmental initiative and authority would reemerge in other social reform suggestions made by Tocqueville. Ultimately, the recommendations of the commission were not accepted, and Tocqueville, as part of a second commission, would write a series of articles in December 1843, to publicize and support a set of revised proposals on emancipation. This effort would also fail. Abolition did not come to the French Empire until 1848.

Early in 1843, Tocqueville authored several letters on the internal situation in France that appeared in the newspaper *Le Siècle*. In addition to condemning the erosion since 1830 of liberty of association and freedom of the press, he discussed the materialism and individualism that marked the July Monarchy, showing how they led to political apathy and a reflexive fear of any current disorder. The more distant threat, he argued, arose from increasing economic and social inequality and the growing grievances and weight of the working classes. In one of his letters, he returned specifically to the gap between the industrial owners and the industrial workers that he had addressed in his 1840 *Democracy*. "[In industrial society] capital is concentrated in a few hands; the profits of those providing work is disproportionate to the worker's wage; the worker is in a position from which it is hard to escape, for he is situated at a great social distance from his employer, and is dependent on him. Such shocking disparities cannot exist for too long in one society without producing a deep malaise."[30] Extreme inequalities could not be long sustained. Class conflict and revolution were the likely results. He had once again named the problem, but did not yet offer many specific solutions.

In 1844, Tocqueville with several friends bought the newspaper *Le Commerce*, with the purpose of giving a voice to an alternative political viewpoint. He took editorial control and, in July 1844, wrote a statement of the political and economic program he hoped to pursue. Over the next few months, he also contributed several articles. The venture proved unsuccessful financially and was abandoned in June 1845. Some uncertainty remains about which pieces actually came from Tocqueville, but his participation seemed to include articles on administrative centralization, religion and the liberty of teaching, increasing inequality and poverty, and rising class antagonism. To address those economic and social issues, Tocqueville proposed several specific reforms, including free public education for children of the poor, broader political rights, credit associations, mutual aid societies, savings banks (under the control of workers), government supported hospitals, and direct public aid to the poor.[31]

After the electoral victory of the conservatives in 1847, Tocqueville attempted, with a few political allies, to form a new opposition called the Young Left. He drafted part of a manifesto to announce and publicize the platform of this new group. Essential goals included slowly extending the circle of political rights to involve the lower classes in politics, making the intellectual and material fate of the working classes the principal concern of legislative action, equalizing public charges and ending fiscal inequalities, and assuring the legal equality and material well-being of the poor. Behind these measures, Tocqueville apparently had three familiar, general ends in mind: the revival of political life, the alleviation of poverty, and the defense of property rights.[32]

To attain the purposes of the manifesto, a related "Fragment for a Social Policy" listed a number of detailed proposals, clustered around both direct and indirect ways of aiding the poor. "It is impossible that inequality of fortunes not be felt in taxation as in everything," Tocqueville observed. "What we at least ought to tend towards is that it be felt as little as possible. We can arrive at this result by adopting these ... rules. 1. Exempt the poorest people from taxation, that is those for whom the burden is heaviest. 2. Do not tax necessities, because then everyone is obliged to pay and the poor are burdened. 3. When taxes bear on things that are necessary or very useful, make them very low for everyone, so that they are almost as indifferent for poor people as for rich people. 4. When the tax is high, try to make it proportional to the wealth of the taxpayer. ...

"What could be done for the lower class may be divided into several categories. ... Let us see what [the] direct means [of coming to the aid of the poor] would be. By establishing institutions which were intended particularly for use by the poor man, which he could use to educate himself, to enrich himself, such as savings banks, credit institutions, free schools, restrictive laws about the duration of work, asylums, workshops, mutual aid societies. Finally by coming directly to his aid and comforting his poverty, with the resources from taxation: hospitals, charity bureaus, poor-taxes, distribution of commodities, of work, of money. Finally, three means of coming to the aid of the lower classes: 1. Exempt him from part of the public burdens or at least only burden him proportionately. 2. Put within his reach the institutions that will let him get by and help him. 3. Come to his aid and assist him directly with his needs. ...[The] true meaning of the revolution is equality, the more equal distribution of the goods of this world. [The] new governments or the classes newly brought to power cannot maintain themselves except by doing all that is possible in this sense."[33]

From these successive letters, articles, and drafts emerged a list of distinct reform measures envisaged by Tocqueville to meet the social and economic challenges he saw in France in the 1840s. During this decade he also showed an interest in alleviating certain social problems on the departmental level, where he concentrated on the privations facing poor or abandoned children, orphans, and single mothers. From 1843 to 1846, he undertook considerable research and submitted four reports to the departmental council recognizing the need on the local level for legal charity to provide clothing, food, education, and other basics to children and single mothers facing poverty. He also called for similar reforms on the national level.[34]

In September 1848, Tocqueville delivered an impassioned speech against the supposed "Right to Work." Despite his earlier statements of support for reforms to favor the working classes, he strongly rejected any state endorsement of the right to work, of guaranteed employment by the government as employer of last resort. He saw such a policy as a precursor to socialism, fiercely denouncing socialist ideas in ways that would soon recur in his *Recollections* and foreshadowed *The Old Regime*. The government, Tocqueville asserted, must use all its means to come "to the rescue of all who suffer, of all, who, after having exhausted all their resources, would be reduced to misery if the State did not lend a hand." But a guarantee of employment would ultimately turn the state into sole industrialist and proprietor and lead to socialism. And socialism, for Tocqueville, meant equality without liberty and the end of private property.[35]

In the writings we have just examined, certain themes recur. As he pondered social issues, Tocqueville kept returning to the importance of property rights and ownership; the goal of reducing extreme inequality and supporting economic and social mobility; the promotion of cooperation among classes and a broader social vision (less collective individualism); the stimulation of political life; the achievement of social and political stability; the best means to help the most vulnerable; and the appropriate role – necessary, but strictly limited – of government. Such principles remained essential to his social and political theory.

Tocqueville's suggested reform measures of the 1840s remained quite moderate: he wanted to motivate and move those unwilling to face developing social and economic problems and yet not fall himself into radical positions. His approach was usually gradualist, often using such words as *tending toward* or *slowly* achieving a particular goal. After the violence of June 1848, he also moved somewhat to the right and became more cautious. Tocqueville, it may be said, pursued moderate reform, in part, for conservative purposes. In May 1848, he declared to Lord Radnor: "We are in the midst of a general revolution of the civilized peoples .... There is only one way to avert and attenuate this revolution, which is to do everything that is possible to ameliorate the lot of the people before being forced to do so."[36] And we need to remember that many of his social reform proposals remained unsigned or unpublished, appearing only in drafts and private papers. Any recognition of Tocqueville as a moderate social reformer has been badly undermined by such reticence and lack of transparency. Nonetheless, his suggested reforms are quite significant; they presume a substantial role by government in the economic life of a nation.

The Role of Government

Tocqueville's warnings about administrative centralization, excessive intrusion of the state or central power in the life of society, and the danger of the new democratic despotism are well known. But such impassioned pleas should not blind readers to a second message woven throughout his thinking and writing. The social reform measures we have noted, for alleviating poverty, shrinking extreme inequalities, restraining the excesses of industrialization, as well as reforming prisons and abolishing slavery, required legislative action and a vigorous government.

In addition, one of Tocqueville's fundamental ideas for preserving liberty in democratic societies demanded efforts by government and leaders to regulate, direct, moderate, and educate the democracy.[37] The range of suggested means to achieve this goal involved not only political or structural mechanisms, such as independent localities, associations, expanded suffrage, and other measures to broaden public participation and support the practice of liberty; it also involved less widely recognized reform measures, such as aid for the destitute, changes in taxation policy and inheritance laws, and means to share both the material and nonmaterial good things of life more equitably.

Tocqueville's broader analysis of democratic dangers and remedies, as well as his economic views and moderate reform proposals, inevitably pose a key question. What is the appropriate role of government in democratic societies? As early as 1830, Tocqueville raised this issue in a letter to Charles Stoffels. "[The] only task that remains for the government is to seek to put itself at the head of [the inescapable inclination of our century] in order to direct it, to lavish instruction itself in order to be sure that instruction will not become a murderous weapon in other hands."[38] This momentous charge did not imply a sickly government.

Tocqueville struck a similar, if somewhat different, tone in reflections included in notes from his 1835 journey to England. "How one should conceive of society's obligations to its members. Is society obliged, as we think in France, to guarantee the individual and to create his well-being? Or is not its only duty rather to give the individual easy and sure means to guarantee it for himself and to create his own well-being? ... Practical discussion on this subject. Gradual introduction of the English and American principle that, in truth, is only the *general principle of free peoples*. Precautions that must be taken to preserve a strong central power."[39] Here, Tocqueville seemed inclined toward a government sufficiently strong to open paths for individual activity and achievement, but not so bloated as to attempt to direct everything.

He made his position clearer in the 1840 *Democracy*, where he urged action to help industrial workers facing recurring economic crises and intractable poverty. "This state of dependency and misery in which a part of the industrial population finds itself in our time is an exceptional fact contrary to all that surrounds it; but for this very reason, there is no fact more serious, or one that better deserves to attract the attention of the legislator."[40] "Industry," he observed in another passage, "usually gathers a multitude of men in the same place; it establishes new and complicated relationships among them. It exposes them to great and sudden shifts between abundance and poverty, during which public tranquility is threatened. It can happen finally that these works compromise the health and even the lives of those who profit from them or of those who devote themselves to them. Thus, the industrial class [the class of industrialists] has more need to be regulated, supervised and restrained than all the other classes, and it is natural that the attributions of the government grow with it."[41] Note here Tocqueville's worry about concentrated power, not in public hands (the central government), but in private hands (the industrial class); either one was unacceptable to Tocqueville. For him, potential abuses of power in democracies were private as well as public.

In draft fragments, Tocqueville approached the subject more theoretically, but with the same definitive conclusion. "The French believe that centralization is French. They are wrong; it is democratic, and I dare to predict that all peoples whose social state will be the same and who follow only the instincts that this social state suggests will arrive at the point where we are. ... A strong and intelligent central power is one of the first political necessities in centuries of equality. Acknowledge it boldly." In the margin, he added: "Contained within certain limits, centralization is a necessary fact, and I add that it is a fact about which we must be glad."[42]

In his penultimate chapter, summarizing his 1840 work, he made the same point, this time not in a draft, but in his text. "It results from the very constitution of democratic nations and from their needs that, among them, the power of the sovereign must be more uniform, more centralized, more extensive, more penetrating, more powerful than elsewhere. Society there is naturally more active and stronger; the individual, more subordinate and weaker. The one does more; the other less; that is inevitable. ... It is at the very same time necessary and desirable that the central power that directs a democratic people be active and powerful. It is not a matter of making it weak or indolent, but only of preventing it from abusing its agility and strength."[43] Here was Tocqueville's fundamental position. Government must be sufficiently strong to be effective, but needed to stay within strict limits in the exercise of power.

As Tocqueville wrote the 1840 *Democracy*, he drafted two brief segments concerning the role of government, each of which addressed special examples. The first involved the American approach, the mixed system already noted, to "works that do not precisely have a national character, but whose execution is very difficult." In the United States, he wrote, the government takes part in such endeavors, not leaving them solely to private associations. From that observation, Tocqueville drew his general conclusion. "Men who live in democratic centuries have more need than others to be allowed to do things by themselves, and more than others, they sometimes need things to be done for them. That depends on circumstances.

The greatest art of government in democratic countries consists in clearly distinguishing the circumstances and acting according to how circumstances lead it."[44]

The second draft fragment addressed the democratic tendencies to emphasize the practical applications of science and to favor middling intellectual standards. To solve these related problems, Tocqueville urged government support of the theoretical sciences and of learned societies. "Of academic institutions under democracy. An academy having the purpose of keeping minds on a certain path, of imposing a method on them, is contrary to the genius of democracy; it is an aristocratic institution. An academy having the goal of making the men who apply themselves to the arts or to the sciences famous and giving them at State expense the comfort and leisure that the democratic social state often denies to them, is an institution that can be not to the taste of a democratic nation, but one that is never contrary to and can sometimes be necessary to the existence of a democracy. It is an eminently democratic institution. Of the need for paid learned bodies in democracies. This need increases as peoples turn toward democracy. This truth understood with difficulty by the democracy. Opposite natural inclination that you must combat. The Americans give way to it."[45]

A fragment dated 1848 posed the key question: "What is a democratic government? It is a government which, instead of limiting human freedom, comes to its aid in a thousand different ways; a government which, instead of setting limits to freedom, opens up all sorts of vistas; instead of setting up new obstacles, finishes destroying those blocking the way; a government which does not steer freedom but instead provides the knowledge and resources that allow it to [incomplete]. It is a government which makes it possible for every citizen, even the humblest, to act with as much independence as the highest citizen, and put his independence to equally good use."[46] This definition is not a description of minimal government.

In his manuscripts for *The Old Regime*, Tocqueville returned to the issue of legal charity and once again urged appropriate legislative action. "I know everything there is to say against government charity, but that does not stop me from thinking that it [sometimes] becomes necessary.... From the moment when the rich classes no longer have a direct and permanent interest and a strict duty to come to the aid of the poor classes, and preserve them from the most extreme hardships, it is necessary that the law force them to do so. When next the aristocracy proper itself gives way, ... legislation that provides for the most pressing needs of the poor is still more necessary. And when finally the last traces of the old hierarchy of ranks are eliminated and individuals are isolated from one another, independent and mutually indifferent, such legislation becomes absolutely indispensable. Democratic society, government charity, two things which go together."[47]

So Tocqueville, as a thinker and active political figure, did not argue for minimal governmental involvement in society. He should not be seen as a theorist who wanted government simply to stand aside and endorse a laissez-faire policy. Tocqueville leaves his readers with a dilemma. In his writings, he calls repeatedly for governmental leadership and for legislative action. But at the same time, throughout his works, he warns habitually against excessive government and the concentration of power in the hands of the central authority.

Tocqueville wanted a vigorous central power, capable of countering the democratic weaknesses and dangers he presented in his works. But, for him, government also needed emphatically to stay within a strictly defined sphere of powers and responsibility. To go beyond that legitimate arena meant the path to democratic tyranny. His persistent moderation, his avoidance of extremes, becomes apparent once again. About government intervention, he offered not ringing endorsements, but tempered judgments. Here was the nub of the greatest art of government in democratic times.

Justice Revisited

As we have noted, for Tocqueville justice stood as perhaps the fundamental argument in favor of democracy. Greater justice also served as one of the basic goals of his proposals for social reform. For more than twenty years, Tocqueville's understanding of what constituted justice remained consistent. In 1835 he responded to a rebuke from Nassau William Senior over an assertion made in the first volume of *Democracy in America*. In England, Tocqueville had written, "the good of the poor had ultimately been sacrificed to that of the rich." In his dissent, Senior read *good* as *wealth*. Tocqueville took a much broader view of *good*. "I had wished to speak, myself, of all the things that can concur in the well-being of life: consideration, political rights, ease of obtaining justice, pleasures of the mind, and a thousand other things that contribute indirectly to happiness."[48] For him, a more just society implied the greater availability of the good things of life, both tangible and intangible.

Tocqueville repeated this viewpoint twelve years later in a letter to Prosper Enfantin, one of the contributors to *Le Commerce* and former leader of the romantic socialist sect of the Saint-Simonians. Tocqueville acknowledged receipt in 1847 of Enfantin's latest book, and although the differences between the two men were many, he signaled an important point of agreement with Enfantin. "There reigns throughout your book an acute feeling of the miseries of the poor and an impulse toward all that could equalize the sum total of happiness that men enjoy in this world. I also believe that the meaning of the long revolution that our fathers saw begin and that we will not see end is a greater development of equality on the earth and a more and more equal sharing of the good things that it offers."[49]

In 1856, a few months before his death, Tocqueville made a similar declaration in an epistle to Sophie Swetchine. "I am very much of your opinion that a more equal distribution of goods [good things] and rights in this world is the greatest aim that those who conduct human affairs can have in view."[50] Here is a remarkable joining in Tocqueville's mind and writing of the economic and political dimensions of a desired justice. And notice the obligation placed upon those who led society. This persistent vision of what can be called distributive justice in its broadest sense arose in part from what Tocqueville considered a contemporary expansion of Christian morality. We have already cited his 1843 letter to Gobineau endorsing "the idea that *all* men have a right to certain goods, to certain enjoyments, and that the first moral obligation is to obtain those things for them."[51]

Another way to grasp Tocqueville's conception of justice is to recall his considerable list of what might be called *affronts to justice*. In his American travel diaries and in the 1835 *Democracy*, Tocqueville depicted and denounced the cruel treatment in the United States of Native Americans and of African Americans, both slave and free.[52] His journey notes in England and Ireland contained the descriptions already cited of the appalling living conditions of English factory workers and the Irish poor. And in the pages of the 1840 *Democracy*, he exposed what he bluntly labeled as the brutalization of those who labored in the new industries.

In addition to eyewitness accounts of mistreatment, cruelty, and degradation, Tocqueville also constructed several artificial portraits that encapsulated some of the injustices described in his books. One, in the 1835 *Democracy*, involved an imagined victim of tyranny of the majority. "When a man...suffers from an injustice in the United States, to whom do you want [him] to appeal? To public opinion?

That is what forms the majority. To the legislative body? It represents the majority and blindly obeys it. To the executive power? It is named by the majority and serves it as a passive instrument. To the police? The police are nothing other than the majority under arms. To the jury? The jury is the majority vested with the right to deliver judgments. The judges themselves, in certain states, are elected by the majority. However iniquitous or unreasonable the measure that strikes you may be, you must therefore submit to it."[53]

And in *The Old Regime*, Tocqueville evoked the French peasant, target of unfair treatment and exploitation. "Imagine the French peasant of the eighteenth century.... Look at him..., so passionately in love with the land that he devotes all his savings to buying it at any price. To acquire it he must first pay a fee, not to the government, but to some other local landowners.... Finally, he owns it; he puts his heart into it with his seed. The little piece of dirt that belongs to him in this vast universe fills him with pride and independence. However, there remain the same neighbors who tear him from his fields and force him to work elsewhere without pay. If he wants to defend his crops against their game, these men forbid it; the same men wait for him at the ford to demand a toll. There they are again at the market, where they sell him the right to sell his own crops; and when he returns home, and wants to use what remains of his wheat for himself, the wheat that has grown under his eyes and by his hands, he cannot do so without having it milled in the mill and baked in the oven of these same men. Part of the income of his little property must be used to pay their fees.... Whatever he does, he encounters these troublesome neighbors everywhere. They disturb his pleasure, hinder his work, eat his produce; and when he has finished with them, still others appear, dressed in black, who take the best of his harvest from him. Imagine the situation, the needs, the character, the passions of this man and calculate, if you can, the amount of hatred and envy stored in his heart."[54]

Readers should recognize Tocqueville's insistence on justice.[55] Greater equity is as much an element of his social and political theory as the more familiar warnings about democratic centralization.

Concluding Comments

Why did the twin problems of growing poverty and increasing inequality draw Tocqueville's interest so consistently? And how does his discussion of political economy fit into his broader social and political thinking? Here, we do not need to reproduce his most important economic views or review his proposed package of social reforms. The question at hand is how his ideas about economic developments and social reform, presented in his writings from the 1830s to the 1850s, connect with his distinctive analysis of the nature, advantages, and disadvantages of democracy, and with his program for preserving liberty in the age of equality. For Tocqueville, the essential meaning of democracy remained equality of conditions. But industrialization, he realized, threatened to introduce a new and disturbing inequality. The rise of industry brought, among other things, class divisions and poverty. So economic developments challenged his fundamental democratic thesis and put into question his recommendations for promoting the benefits and avoiding the pitfalls of democracy.

One of his goals for reform was to avoid revolution or chronic instability. Efforts to alleviate the plight of the lower classes were needed to counter the more extreme and radical theories of the socialists, who questioned the legitimacy of middle-class wealth and attacked private property. Without reforms, the right of property, which Tocqueville considered essential in civilized society, was put at risk. But Tocqueville's understanding of economic and social dynamics did not simply drive him into a defensive position, urging moderate reforms to blunt the appeal of more radical changes. Tocqueville the moralist had other goals in mind. At times, he explicitly addressed the crushing of the human mind and spirit that came with unrestrained industrialization.

Seeing Manchester in 1835, he remarked in his travel diaries: "What room for the life of the spirit can a man have who works for about twelve hours a day every day except Sunday?"[56] Echoing Adam Smith, he made a similar point in the 1840 *Democracy*. "What should you expect," he wrote, "from a man who has used twenty years of his life making pinheads? ... When a worker has in this way consumed a considerable portion of his existence, his thought has stopped forever near the daily object of his labor; his body has contracted certain fixed habits that he is no longer allowed to give up. In a word, he no longer belongs to himself."[57]

Tocqueville had witnessed and learned about genuine injustices that required solutions. He had also developed a strong sense of distributive justice. His suggested program to address poverty served a fundamental moral purpose, the more equitable sharing of the good things of the earth. Some individuals should not be left completely vulnerable, dependent, and brutalized for the benefit of others.

And as we know, the *good things* meant, for Tocqueville, not only material benefits, such as comfort and security, but also benefits of mind and spirit, such as education and the opportunity to experience and enjoy the intangible pleasures of life.

Tocqueville worried as well that inequality and poverty undermined the possibility of democratic freedom. Greater equity would allow for genuine and effective participation in public life. For Tocqueville, extreme inequality and grinding poverty made the practice of liberty impossible and turned liberty itself into a sham. Participatory democracy required citizens who had not only nominal rights, but also the capacity – the time, energy, enlightenment, and breadth of mind – to exercise those rights. Civic responsibility, public virtues, and development of a sense of citizenship came primarily from putting rights and liberty into action. But marginalized individuals and classes were unable to participate in the civic arena in any meaningful way. For democratic freedom, as Tocqueville understood it, rough equality (of opportunity at least) and the alleviation of extreme poverty were necessary preconditions.

All of this related to Tocqueville's larger goal of moderating and enlightening democratic peoples and turning them toward the advantages and away from the disadvantages of democracy. Equality of condition, joined with liberty, would, in Tocqueville's eyes, elevate human souls and spur human grandeur. Always at the core of Tocqueville's thinking was found the moral dimension of his social, political, and economic theory.

7

Tocqueville's Reputation and Continuing Relevance

Initial Success and Enduring Interest

Any study of Tocqueville's thinking and writing needs to recount briefly the story of the remarkable success and lasting reputation of his two major books, *Democracy in America* and *The Old Regime*. In 1835, leading academic, social, and political figures, who, at the time, constituted the French reading public of serious works,[1] greeted *Democracy in America* and its young author with acclaim. "Well," declared Gosselin, the unsuspecting publisher, "it seems you have written a masterpiece." Seven printings of the 1835 *Democracy* followed in the next four years, even before the second volume of the work appeared. The 1835 volume was widely reviewed and mostly praised in France, England, the United States, and elsewhere. The reaction to the 1840 *Democracy* was more qualified, but still largely positive. And the reception of *The Old Regime* in 1856 followed the same pattern. The first edition sold out in two months; within three years, four additional printings appeared and nine thousand copies were sold. Once again, mostly laudatory reviews appeared in France, England, Germany, and elsewhere; and because of *The Old Regime*, Tocqueville also became known in Russia.[2] Such are the minimal details.

Certain judgments are even more impressive. One prominent American political scientist has labeled Tocqueville's *Democracy* as "at once the best book ever written on democracy and the best book ever written about America."[3] François Furet, arguably the most preeminent historian of the French Revolution in the last half of the twentieth century, called Tocqueville's *Old Regime* "the most important book of the entire French historiography of the French Revolution."[4] Commentators, whatever their political perspective and despite any criticisms, reservations, or corrections they may offer, seem almost universally to value the eloquence, originality, and theoretical brilliance of Tocqueville's writings.

Contrary to a widespread misconception, interest in Tocqueville and *Democracy in America* has remained persistent in the United States since the 1830s.[5] At the turn of the twentieth century, when his reputation supposedly went into decline, several significant new editions of the work, both scholarly and popular, were published and reprinted, in 1898, 1899, 1900, and 1904. At that time, *Democracy* continued also to be excerpted and used in schools to teach young Americans about their own political institutions. But if Tocqueville's standing in America did not go into eclipse by the end of the nineteenth century, an undeniable upsurge in interest did occur, beginning in the 1930s and increasing after World War II. The American fascination with Tocqueville and his first great book has only deepened during the last half century.

Since 2000, three completely new translations of *Democracy in America* have been published in the United States, plus a further one in England. And new translations and critical editions of *The Old Regime* and *Recollections* appeared in America in 1998 and 2016 respectively.[6] In addition, Tocqueville's travel notes to America, England, and Ireland are available; and articles, monographs, compilations of extensive excerpts from Tocqueville's correspondence and other writings, as well as collections of essays by Tocqueville specialists, continue to appear in great numbers. What has been called a "cottage industry" seems to be proceeding without letup.

Several shifts in the American appreciation of Tocqueville should be noted. First, *The Old Regime* received relatively little attention in the United States until the late twentieth century; for Americans, Tocqueville was the author of *Democracy in America*. Second, American editors since the end of the nineteenth century have recognized that the New World republic has changed profoundly since Tocqueville's visit in 1831–2. Daniel Coit Gilman, the most scholarly editor among those who presented new editions of *Democracy* at the turn of the twentieth century, enumerated in 1898 the undeniable transformations in the United States since the publication of Tocqueville's book six decades earlier. He listed continental expansion, significant population growth, broader ethnic and racial diversity, great fortunes and powerful captains of industry, celebrated cultural and educational institutions, more complex governmental institutions, the beginnings of an American empire, and the new international role of the United States. Gilman even pointed in 1898 to a wide gap between rich and poor and wondered whether Tocqueville's concept of growing equality still fit the American republic. Nonetheless, like other editors since the 1830s, he stressed the lasting importance and value of Tocqueville's book as a study of American society, politics, and culture.

Third, throughout the nineteenth century and up to the mid-twentieth, commentators concentrated almost exclusively on the 1835 volume of Tocqueville's book, focusing on his analysis of American political and legal institutions. Readers regarded the 1840 *Democracy* as overly deductive, too abstract, and not really about America. By the mid-twentieth century, however, attention shifted markedly to the second part of Tocqueville's work. Americans, especially those newly interested in American studies and American civilization, were increasingly drawn to the social, cultural, and psychological dimensions of Tocqueville's 1840 portrait of democratic societies. And instead of seeing Tocqueville primarily as an analyst of America, readers in the United States, including American historians, began to appreciate the larger scope of Tocqueville's writings, including *The Old Regime*. They have increasingly focused on Tocqueville as a social and political theorist, who dissected the varied consequences, both positive and negative, of democracy and who examined broad social and political change within French and European, as well as American contexts. His canvass was clearly not limited to the New World republic.

Fourth, since the last decades of the twentieth century, Tocqueville has been embraced in the United States especially by more conservative political theorists, who are captivated particularly by his portrait of the new democratic despotism, his critique of centralization and excessive government, his emphasis on the role of religion, and his warnings about the possible shortcomings of modern democratic societies, including moral decline, individual alienation and rootlessness, and the weakening of shared values. Strikingly, Tocqueville has taken on the coloration of successive generations of American historians, political scientists, and sociologists. During the Progressive era in the early twentieth century, he was made into a fellow Progressive. By the mid-twentieth century, he became the embodiment of a consensus spokesman, standing for the shared liberal tradition then thought to characterize American civilization. And by the late twentieth century, with more widespread pessimism about the modern world, Tocqueville became a voice for profoundly conservative views.

A fundamental appeal of *Democracy* for New World republicans has always been Tocqueville's largely positive depiction of American institutions and of the American model. He considered the example of the United States important for France and indeed for the rest of the modern world. And, like other peoples, Americans enjoy being praised and seen as a nation at the forefront of global development. Yet, paradoxically, Tocqueville also speaks to the changing worries that Americans at different times have had about their own society, politics, and culture. For each generation, he is able to address the very things that most trouble Americans and to suggest possible remedies. To a large degree, this ability to speak to shifting concerns explains why Tocqueville is read so much in the United States today. His *Democracy* is probably now studied less for what he praised about the American republic than for what he warned against. Contemporary readings, matching the mood, are darker than earlier ones.

Ironically, Tocqueville's near oblivion between the 1870s and the mid-twentieth century applies rather to France than to the United States. In *Tocqueville and the French*, Françoise Mélonio points out the disappearance after the 1870s, and until 1951, of any new editions of *Democracy in America* in France.[7] French critics saw Tocqueville's portrait of the American republic as largely inaccurate and outdated. For the French, by the closing decades of the nineteenth century, Tocqueville's reputation rested primarily on *The Old Regime*, not on *Democracy in America*. And remarkably, according to Mélonio, *The Old Regime* accomplished exactly what Tocqueville had hoped. The book precipitated a revival of the desire for liberty in France.

A few important works about Tocqueville did appear in France at the turn of the twentieth century. And by the 1950s, French interest in Tocqueville, reflecting the trajectory in America, revived dramatically, starting with renewed appreciation of the 1835 *Democracy*, then embracing the 1840 volume. The authoritative and enormous project, now nearing its end, of the publication of the complete works of Tocqueville was launched in 1951. And by the 1970s, largely due to the influence of Furet, *The Old Regime* became a renewed focus of attention. For many French intellectuals, Tocqueville's ideas took the place of a Marxist analysis in eclipse. From France in 1984 also came the first full biography of Tocqueville, written by André Jardin, one of the premier Tocqueville specialists of the twentieth century. Mélonio describes this entire process of rediscovery and traces, as well, the familiar characteristic of successive readings of Tocqueville.

In France, as in the United States, he has been claimed at various times by commentators on the right, left, and center, who have in turn emphasized different and sometimes competing elements of his books.

Tocqueville's *Democracy*, translated by Henry Reeve, appeared in England simultaneously with the French publication and turned the author into a famous and much sought-after figure among English intellectuals, political leaders, and aristocrats. The same story of translation and praise occurred in England when *The Old Regime* appeared in 1856. England became Tocqueville's second country and has remained a keystone of appreciation for Tocqueville's thinking and writing. From England, for example, came the reflections of John Stuart Mill on *Democracy in America* (both 1835 and 1840), perhaps the best reviews ever written on Tocqueville's book and certainly the commentaries most prized by Tocqueville for capturing his essential message; the first complete biography of Tocqueville originally written in English;[8] and a long and continuing list of other monographs, articles, and editions, including the 2003 translation already mentioned.

Interest in Tocqueville's books has not been restricted to Europe and the New World. In 1868, the Meiji Restoration in Japan ended the Shogunate, restored the authority of the Emperor, and began the story of the modern nation. Not long after, in the 1870s and 1880s, a few Japanese thinkers and political figures began to read Tocqueville, especially Fukuzawa Yukichi, who became the primary standard bearer of his generation for the Japanese study of Tocqueville. Certain chapters of the 1835 *Democracy* were translated as early as 1873, and a translation of the entire first volume appeared in 1881–2. Since the end of the nineteenth century, Japanese interest has continued, producing a long and distinguished line of Tocqueville specialists who have addressed a variety of themes, including the unfolding of equality, the importance of liberties – especially freedom of the press – the influence of democracy on public spirit and patriotism, the issue of centralization, and the emergence of democratic mores – especially changes in family relationships and values. More recently, some Japanese Tocqueville scholars have also turned their attention to *The Old Regime* and explored the similarities and differences between the French Revolution and the Meiji Restoration/Revolution. And in 2008, Reiji Matsumoto, probably the most outstanding Japanese Tocqueville scholar of his generation, produced a full four-volume translation into Japanese of Tocqueville's *Democracy in America*.[9]

The tradition of Tocqueville studies is well over a century old in Japan; China, by contrast, presents a very different story. Strong interest in Tocqueville's ideas has come late in China, developing only since the 1980s. Nonetheless, in the last few decades, significant works by Chinese specialists on Tocqueville have appeared, including various editions of his major works and selections from his travel notes, from his correspondence, and from the incomplete drafts of *The Old Regime*. A Chinese translation by Dong Guoliang of the entire *Democracy in America* was published in 1988. If Japanese scholars have focused primarily on *Democracy*, Chinese readers much more recently have concentrated on *The Old Regime*, first published in a complete Chinese translation in 1991. Tocqueville's study of the French Revolution, its causes and aftermath, offers two alternative questions relevant to contemporary China. First, given increasing prosperity, rising expectations, and the beginnings of reform, how can a nation (China) avoid a revolution and the collapse of a regime such as occurred in France in 1789? Or, second, how can a nation (China) regain and maintain stability after the jarring revolutionary changes of Mao Zedong and Deng Xiaoping?[10] These queries, posed by Tocqueville for France, apply only too well to China at the beginning of the twenty-first century.

Interest in Tocqueville continues to spread. Several recent volumes now offer collections of essays that relate his ideas and approach to a variety of non-Western nations, beyond the examples of China and Japan, such as Korea, Burma, Argentina, and other countries in Africa, Latin America, and the Middle East.[11] So Tocqueville scholarship is flourishing in the world.

How can we explain such persistent and broadening attention to works of political and social theory and historical analysis written in the middle decades of the nineteenth century? Such growing interest is itself an indication of the value of Tocqueville's thinking and writing. And recurring timeliness serves as another mark of his legacy. As noted, the complexity and richness of Tocqueville's analysis seem to engage succeeding generations as though he were a contemporary. His treatment of modern democratic society – with its benefits and dangers – seems to work as a mirror for the varied perspectives and concerns of consecutive cohorts of commentators and general readers.

In addition, some of Tocqueville's defining ways of thinking and writing continue to draw attention, including his preference for complexity and nuance, his originality, his habit of constant reconsideration, his powers of analysis, his ability to pose dilemmas and wrestle with ambiguities, his sensitivity to national and historical contexts, and his focus on mores and social state as essential features for understanding modern society.

He was also able to raise essential questions that have not lost their pertinence. How can liberty be preserved in the age of equality? What are the main causes for the success or failure, stability or instability, prosperity or poverty, freedom or despotism of a given nation? What are the meanings and consequences of democracy? How can we get the best and avoid the worst from democracy? How best to promote the dispersal of power and escape centralization in modern society? What measures should be taken to assure liberties that are real and not hollow? What must we do to protect individual independence in the face of the majority, the mass, public opinion, or any gathering of the whole social power? How can we uphold shared values and higher moral purposes in societies increasingly turned toward materialism and commercial values? What is the appropriate role of religion in democratic societies? How can we encourage public engagement, a vigorous civic life, and better awareness of shared rights and responsibilities? And how can human beings in today's world be persuaded to take responsibility for their own social and political future? Tocqueville's reputation may rest more on the issues he raised than on his proposed solutions.

Resonances

Yet another indication of Tocqueville's continuing relevance and importance as a social and political theorist are the resonances that occur between Tocqueville and other prominent political thinkers of the late nineteenth, twentieth, and into the twenty-first centuries. Before proceeding with a few thumbnail and highly impressionistic sketches of similarities, we need to register three fundamental caveats. First, by briefly painting some parallels between Tocqueville and a few other social and political theorists, we are not attempting to evaluate the accuracy of Tocqueville's ideas or those of the other writers mentioned. The question of whose analysis is more correct, coherent, defensible, or persuasive is not the issue here. Second, we are not assuming that the theorists cited used Tocqueville as a source or based their ideas on his; these thinkers are not necessarily *echoing* Tocqueville in either sense. If some found his ideas compatible and helpful, others pointedly criticized or dissented from him. The discussion that follows simply attempts to call attention to a few significant affinities in issues addressed, dilemmas posed, and remedies imagined. And finally, the following remarks are intended only to sketch a few noteworthy similarities; they are not at all meant to be examinations of the political thinkers mentioned, or complete explorations of parallels with Tocqueville. Interested readers, we hope, will pursue their own more thorough study of the pairings presented here.

John Stuart Mill (1806–72)

John Stuart Mill, Tocqueville's contemporary and probably the most important political philosopher in the English-speaking world in the nineteenth century, is best known for *On Liberty* (1859) and *Considerations on Representative Government* (1861). His connection with Tocqueville rested upon a friendship that quickly arose after an initial meeting in England in 1835. As we have noted, Mill wrote, for both volumes of *Democracy in America*, perceptive, measured and laudatory reviews, highly appreciated by Tocqueville. It was also at Mill's request that Tocqueville in 1836 first wrote an essay about the *ancien régime* and the French Revolution. The two men corresponded faithfully until the early 1840s, when Tocqueville, with a display of chauvinism and bellicosity about French foreign policy, shocked Mill into silence for several years.[12]

The two political theorists are probably best known as brilliant spokesmen for liberty. Mill centered perhaps more on the passive or negative liberty of being left alone than Tocqueville, who insisted on the practice of liberty, on the actual exercise or use of rights. Nonetheless, both championed essential rights or freedoms, especially of expression, and argued for expanded suffrage and broad political participation, including, in Mill's case, voting rights for women. Both also stressed the importance of civic engagement as a way to develop a sense of citizenship, to broaden the horizons and develop the full potential of individuals, and to strengthen individual independence.

But the link between Mill and Tocqueville involves more than a few broad parallels in ideas. They shared ways of thinking, particularly the intellectual habits of avoiding absolutes, honoring contexts, and seeking how best to balance competing principles. Although Tocqueville does not seem to reflect any significant influences from Mill, the English thinker credited Tocqueville in his *Autobiography* with several noteworthy lessons. Most important was Mill's reassessment, as he read Tocqueville's 1835 book, of the idea of representative democracy as a way to soften some of the worst dangers of direct democracy. Mill later pushed this concept far beyond Tocqueville's treatment and ended by proposing weighted voting, allowing various elites to have plural votes. This approach violated the fundamental principle of equality; and Tocqueville believed that no political, legal, or constitutional system could contravene this principle and long endure in the modern democratic age.

Apparently, Tocqueville also broadened Mill's thinking about local liberties and centralization. *Democracy in America* alerted Mill to the potential dangers of excessive centralization and persuaded him about the possible advantages of greater local control, assuming the principle of representation and a more educated and experienced citizenry. Perhaps Mill also found, in Tocqueville's concept of tyranny of the majority and its 1840 transformation into the despotism of public or mass opinion, reinforcement of his own ideas about the oppressive power of public opinion in modern society. Mill certainly repeated the term *tyranny of the majority* in his essay *On Liberty*. The two men parted ways on the influence of religion, however. For Mill, religion played a major role in shaping a repressive public opinion. For Tocqueville, on the other hand, religion, as a support for moral values, served as an essential restraint on some of the worst possible excesses of democracy.

This brief discussion of the connection between the two friends needs to recognize Mill's complaint, as a notable economic theorist, that Tocqueville did not adequately appreciate the work of English political economists. Despite that reproach, Tocqueville did, of course, share much of Mill's critique of the contemporary economic system, although he never went so far as to declare himself a socialist, as Mill did. He also shared Mill's interest in the problem of poverty, its causes and the reforms that might be needed to alleviate want. However, compared to Mill's early advocacy of women's rights, Tocqueville's blindness about women's full equality and legitimate voice in political life remains deeply troubling. Tocqueville was perfectly content with, and even praised, the situation of white women in America, which was at the time of his visit a kind of "separate but (supposedly) equal," a type of political purdah, a system of legal and political subordination. His admiration for the education, courage, and moral standards of Anglo-American women does not erase the larger limitations of his views on the matter of women's rights.[13]

The extent of Tocqueville's influence on Mill should not be exaggerated. The intent here is not to repeat the myth of the Frenchman as a teacher of Mill, but simply to point to affinities, to highlight some of the ideas and concerns shared by the two contemporaries, and to acknowledge a few key differences as well.[14]

Max Weber (1864–1920)

From one point of view, Max Weber strongly distanced himself from Tocqueville. The rise of the bureaucratic state, he asserted, not the march of democracy, defined the modern world. But his understanding of bureaucracy and its role is not so far from Tocqueville's famous portrait of the new democratic despotism, where the smallest detail of an individual's life is overseen and determined by the clerk. Weber's thesis of bureaucratization dovetails with Tocqueville's fears about the twin democratic dangers of power concentrated in the state and of administrative centralization.

Weber also shared Tocqueville's view that beliefs and attitudes strongly shape economic systems and behavior. For Tocqueville, democratic mores encouraged materialism and the commercialization of all areas of society. For Weber, particular religious beliefs (Protestantism) stimulated the spirit and development of capitalism. For both writers, mores remained at the core of any explanation of historical, social, and even economic change. And Weber's concept of the *ideal type* captured much of the essence of Tocqueville's own approach to the aristocratic and democratic social states.[15]

Hannah Arendt (1906–75)

Hannah Arendt's study of totalitarianism in the modern age follows, to some degree, Tocqueville's portrait of democratic despotism. Each theorist considered the despotism they described as new to the world and as marked by the disappearance of any secondary bodies, such as associations, localities, or other independent groups; civil society withered, and all power was gathered into the hands of the state.

Similarities show in their presentation of the causes of the new despotism, particularly the growing isolation and weakness of individuals in the face of mass society. At the same time, significant differences are apparent in their understanding of key features of modern tyranny. Arendt stressed the role of the leader, the need for a political movement or party, and the importance of racism in shaping totalitarianism. And for Arendt, totalitarianism meant a system of violence and terror. For Tocqueville, democratic despotism, though equally intrusive and suffocating, remained essentially mild or soft, relying less on violence than on providing for the smallest needs and slightest material desires of citizens in order to gain their acquiescence.[16]

Friedrich Hayek (1899–1992)

Friedrich Hayek, Nobel laureate in economics and one of the most influential economists of the twentieth century, is also recognized as a powerful advocate of the free market and critic of the welfare state. Any government intervention to encourage greater social and economic equality or distributive justice, he argued, is ultimately ineffective and destructive of liberty. He greatly admired Tocqueville, and his opposition to government involvement seems almost modeled on Tocqueville's condemnation of administrative centralization and his description of the new democratic despotism that would turn citizens into sheep.

But is Hayek reading or misreading Tocqueville on the issue of government intervention in the economy? Certainly Tocqueville, as we have seen, fiercely rejected socialism and the idea of the tutelary state. At the same time, however, he believed government had a legitimate role – beyond simply providing a safety net – in alleviating the worst features of unrestrained capitalism. Government regulations and policies, especially those regarding taxation and inheritance, could attempt to correct market inequalities. Tocqueville was not a spokesman for the free market.[17]

Michael J. Sandel (1953–)

Michael J. Sandel, a prominent American political scientist, is recognized as a major spokesman for a more communitarian approach in political theory. Several striking parallels emerge when his ideas are placed beside those of Tocqueville. He too worries about the growing gap between rich and poor, the habit of measuring everything in market terms, the abuses of unfettered markets that are neither just nor free, and the tendency toward corrosive individualism and extreme privatism. Sandel insists on the importance, not so much of the individual self, but of the communities and traditions shared by individuals, of the social clusters that shape identities, beliefs, values, and behavior, and that help to define the common good. For him, reasoning together and engaging in civic life are essential; and such activities are best practiced in community, that is, in traditional gatherings, associations, and local or grassroots involvements. This accent on the role of associations and localities is perhaps the clearest similarity to Tocqueville's ideas.[18]

Thomas Piketty (1971–)

Tocqueville's writings describe the providential advance of equality of condition and explore the meanings and varieties of equality. By contrast, Thomas Piketty's book, *Capital in the Twenty-First Century*, presents the problem of *inequality* as a defining feature of the modern world and caused a sensation in the United States when published in 2014.[19] Large quantities of ink were spilled in response, both positive and negative, to his thesis. Unregulated capitalism, he insists, creates arbitrary and increasing inequalities of income and wealth. Capitalism does not automatically self-correct, as orthodox advocates of the free market believe, to produce greater equality and distribute income and wealth more equitably.

Growing inequality, Piketty argues, is especially unavoidable in times of slow growth. And the developed nations, especially in Europe and North America, are returning to the extreme and unsustainable levels of inequality that had prevailed in the late eighteenth century and again in the late nineteenth in Europe. For the United States, in particular, Piketty describes an explosion of inequality since 1980. America, he asserts, now presents a level of inequality similar to that of Europe at the turn of the twentieth century and higher than that of contemporary Europe. Like Piketty, Tocqueville criticized raw capitalism precisely because of the profound inequalities it often caused. Capitalism, for both men, requires regulation or moderation, which in turn demands a degree of government intervention, substantial for Piketty, limited for Tocqueville.

Several other significant resonances surface when Piketty is read with Tocqueville in mind. Both Tocqueville and Piketty praise democracy for its greater justice. For them, democracy brings a more equitable distribution of the good things of the earth. And both writers see gross inequality as dangerous to democracy. Tocqueville, as we know, assumed that a healthy, free, and stable democracy entailed a rough equality of condition with no extreme or fixed inequalities; democracy meant, in part, genuine social and economic mobility. For him, it also implied a meaningful political voice, not simply an empty right to vote, but the possibility of real participation in civic life, the development of the habits of citizenship, and an emerging sense of the larger public interest. In his writings, Tocqueville sharply condemned the hollow liberty offered by the two Napoleons and what he saw as the selfish and short-sighted rule of the middle class during the July Monarchy. Piketty also worries that extreme inequalities of income and wealth will tear the fabric of democracy by placing real social and political power in the hands of the few who are at the top of the economic pyramid. For him, such concentrated power, something always feared by Tocqueville, threatens to create an empty or false democracy. Echoing Tocqueville, he strongly advocates democracy as broad political participation and civic engagement.

Piketty describes how the most important category of capital assets has changed fundamentally since the eighteenth century, shifting from landholdings to other types of capital. To lessen inequality, he proposes such measures as a global tax on capital and new attention to inheritance laws. Tocqueville also recognized the importance of inheritance laws. But the 1835 *Democracy*, written at a time when the most important capital asset was land, concentrates on laws concerning the inheritance of landed estates, especially the abolition of entail and primogeniture and the requirement, in France, of equal division.[20] As a political figure in the 1840s, Tocqueville continued, as we have seen, to propose estate taxes that would allow for family inheritance, but avoid as well increasingly large and fixed inequalities of wealth from generation to generation.

The two French theorists also wrestle with the links among the social, economic, and political dimensions of equality and the prospects for social and political stability. Tocqueville observed that those who enjoy social democracy will not long accept the lack of political democracy. Piketty reverses the perspective and argues that those who have political democracy will not long endure extreme economic inequality. He warns against the danger of growing social and political unrest in the world.

If, as Piketty asserts, inequality is the defining feature of the modern world, Tocqueville was wrong. His central thesis of the democratic revolution, of the inexorable march of equality, is mistaken. But the discomfort and even alarm caused by Piketty's vision of extreme inequality testifies to the sway of a psychology of equality, to the deep-seated egalitarian mores in today's world. Given this response, Tocqueville was right. The meanings of equality, as Tocqueville knew, are far more varied and complex than can be measured by economic yardsticks.

Concluding Comments

This selective survey of Tocqueville readings, in different nations and as a background for the works of other theorists, provides some intriguing lessons. Tocqueville's *Democracy in America* and *The Old Regime* continue to draw readers, thoughtful attention, and almost universal praise. And Tocqueville's thinking and writing seem to appeal to constantly wider audiences.

His ideas also appear to echo in the works of multiple political thinkers, from different eras and of different political viewpoints. Such parallels reflect not necessarily matters of agreement or disagreement, but shared interests in similar issues, in familiar questions, and sometimes in matching solutions. The resonances between Tocqueville and the writers chosen somewhat arbitrarily for our discussion cluster repeatedly around a few of Tocqueville's most intriguing and original concepts: the power of mores, the meanings of equality, the need for participatory democracy and active liberty, the possible advantages and disadvantages of democracy, the hallmarks of democratic psychology, and especially his dramatic and unforgettable image of the new democratic despotism.

Tocqueville's reputation and relevance are observable over *time*, from the nineteenth to the twenty-first century; over *space* or geography, from Europe and America, to elsewhere in the world; and over *political persuasions*, from right, left, and center. Such a legacy is rare and deserves our careful consideration. We should also remember Tocqueville's own judgment. "I please many people of conflicting opinions, not because they understand me, but because they find in my work, by considering it only from a single side, arguments favorable to their passion of the moment. But I have confidence in the future, and I hope that a day will come when everyone will see clearly what only some perceive today."[21] His words should remind all of his readers and interpreters to practice intellectual humility.

Conclusion

What have we learned about Tocqueville as a social and political theorist? As acknowledged at the outset, an introductory study, necessarily brief, can only examine a selection of themes and complexities in Tocqueville's work. Many topics have only been touched upon, if mentioned at all. Much more could be said, for example, about Tocqueville's sources; his hidden dialogues with such figures as Montesquieu, Burke, or Guizot; his style and use of language (Tocqueville as a writer); Tocqueville as an historian, his view of history, his philosophy of history; his ideas about education; his vision of an ideal republic; his interest in *passions*, especially political and religious; and his exploration of the influence of democracy on literature, the arts, and language.

Despite these silences or near silences, we have witnessed many of Tocqueville's habits of thinking and writing, including his search for new or almost new words to label novel concepts (such as *individualism* and *collective individualism*), his tendency to leave open-ended definitions (most famously, the meaning of democracy), and his decision to present portraits when new names failed to emerge (especially the new democratic despotism). As Tocqueville prepared not only his major works, but also his various reports, essays, and speeches, he also faithfully conducted thorough research, including more innovative techniques, such as travel, interviews, and archival investigation. His thinking is characterized by complexity, balance, and a tight linkage, from one idea to another, which mirrors his belief in the interconnections among all areas of society. By personal and intellectual preference, he strove for moderation and impartiality. As we have noted, he also avoided absolutes or final answers, preferring constant reconsideration of his tentative conclusions.

Other major features of Tocqueville's thought are his insistence on comparison and his emphasis on the contexts of history and nations. By visiting, observing, studying, and comparing a particular society or time, the distinctive features of another country or era would, he believed, emerge the more clearly. Such comparisons, either as pairs or as trios, involving France, America, England, and sometimes Germany, informed the discussion in both *Democracy in America* and *The Old Regime*.

Awareness of self and of his intended audience also marked Tocqueville as an author. Early plans, notes, and successive drafts for his two major books reveal a decided pattern of self-questioning. In his working papers, he tried constantly to remind himself about his essential purposes and the thread of his argument and to find just the right tone and expression in his exposition. Tocqueville always wrote with France and the French reader primarily in mind.[1] He knew how his intended readers thought; and, in order to persuade them, he understood how best to frame his line of reasoning. In the margins of the drafts and manuscript of *Democracy*, for example, he often commented that his initial language was too strong or his wording too dogmatic; he then penned more palatable versions of his text. Tocqueville also enjoyed the tactics of presenting details to encapsulate broader pictures, making unexpected counterintuitive points, challenging received opinions, and offering reverse proofs. Such methods captured the attention of his audience and demonstrated his facility and originality as a thinker.

Knowledge of the thoughts, assumptions, and fears of his countrymen sometimes turned Tocqueville into a *trimmer*, who modified and softened his ideas and expressions in order not to alienate his audience. Perhaps the best example of Tocqueville purposely blunting his message in order to avoid accusations of extremism or excess passion is his decision to have his *Recollections* published only posthumously. He also occasionally dropped or ignored examples that did not fit his fundamental themes. His travel diaries for the American journey, for example, show much greater awareness of the inequalities of wealth, education, class, and skin color that existed in the New World republic than he would admit in *Democracy*, except in the chapter on the three races.[2] His book largely ignored such distinctions and focused instead on equality of condition as the defining American characteristic.[3] So, in some cases, Tocqueville was aware of elements that did not fit his framework. As a theorist, he inevitably made choices, both to make his message more palatable to his readers and to lend coherence to his fundamental themes.

Although Tocqueville purposely avoided definitive conclusions, he sometimes left serious matters unresolved, offering almost contradictory messages. He advanced conflicting points of view, for example, about intellectual and cultural creativity in democratic nations. Would the energy unleashed by democracy stimulate innovation? Or would democratic society succumb to stagnation and fear of change? He also presented opposing treatments of war as both a harbinger of centralization and possible tyranny and a patriotic solution to democratic materialism and individualism. And how broadly and quickly should the right to vote be extended? During much of the 1840s, Tocqueville's position on suffrage remained woefully ambiguous.

Tocqueville also leaves his readers with several troubling blind spots, including his lack of interest in the rights of women, his chauvinism, his embrace of imperialism and colonialism, his willingness to withhold certain rights from the subjugated Algerians, and his proposal to follow immediate emancipation from slavery with a period of apprenticeship or tutelage for the newly freed. His commitment to liberty and endorsement of equality did not always extend to all groups or to all matters.

Tocqueville's thinking and writing predictably show some significant shifts over nearly thirty years. We have traced, for example, such important changes as a growing recognition, between 1835 and 1840, of the connection between democracy and centralization and the emergence of a different concept of the most dangerous despotism threatening democratic society (the new democratic despotism); the replacement, in the 1840s and 1850s, of America by England as the primary point of comparison with France;[4] and, after 1848, Tocqueville's rising awareness and increasingly sharp denunciation of socialism. We have also followed his expanding interest in the problem of poverty, beginning perhaps during his prison research in America, but developing substantially during his journey to England and Ireland in 1835, and accelerating into the 1840s. The chronic poverty and economic insecurity of the industrial working class, he came to realize, seriously threatened social and political stability and put liberty at risk.

Despite such changes, an essential unity remains the hallmark of Tocqueville as a theorist. What we have called his first principles, such as the inevitable advance of democracy, the primacy of mores, the rejection of determinism, and the right of private property, did not change. Nor did his basic purposes. He worked to present an accurate portrait of democratic society, with its potential consequences, both good and bad. He sought to separate the effects of revolution and those of democracy and to explore the causes and consequences of revolution. He strove to blend the spirit of religion and the spirit of liberty and to bring men of good will together to champion both faith and freedom. Above all, he aimed to preserve liberty in the age of equality. And to avoid the dangers and to promote the benefits of democracy, he proposed a distinctive package of suggested policies and approaches. Taken together, Tocqueville's goals and proposals define what he meant by a new political science.

We have examined the major elements of Tocqueville's political program, most essentially: the dispersal of power, or decentralization (vigorous localities, provinces, associations, and other free institutions); the practice of liberty (the use of civil and political rights, civic engagement, and participatory democracy); the strengthening of individual independence (protection against the combined force of the mass, the majority, public or private power, or any expression of society as a whole); and the avoidance of newly emerging, or fixed and extreme inequalities.

As a theorist, Tocqueville posed a nagging dilemma about the appropriate role of government in democratic nations. He is perhaps remembered most for his warning about administrative centralization and excessive government. But he called for a concerted effort to educate, direct, and moderate the people of democratic societies and to ensure, for them, opportunities for democratic participation and the exercise of freedom. His proposed program of remedies for democratic dangers included not only broad institutional and structural recommendations and suggestions for developing healthy mores, but also a package of specific social and economic reforms. Who or what would undertake this effort and set this program in motion? And who or what would protect democratic nations from potential abuses coming from the private sphere, such as the new industrial aristocracy; oppressive, even violent, associations; or the tyrannical majority clothed in democratic authority? Government, as Tocqueville realized, had a legitimate and increasingly necessary function in democratic society. The great puzzle remained where to mark the boundary of fitting public intervention.

Tocqueville's goal of greater equity is often overlooked as part of his program. He rarely used the words *justice* or *injustice* in either *Democracy in America* or *The Old Regime*. But in his books, letters, and other writings, he called on occasion for a more equitable sharing of the good things of the earth and denounced the injustices he witnessed. His desire to avoid new inequalities, to promote genuine rather than hollow liberty, and to assure participatory democracy, led him in the 1840s toward significant social reform proposals. Tocqueville's consistency went beyond the elements of his theory; it also included the correlation between his ideas as a writer and his recommendations as a political figure.

With his program, Tocqueville aimed to open the path to reaching free, stable, and prosperous democratic societies. His efforts had broad application in the modern world, but France remained his primary target. He wanted to understand and cure French social and political instability, to end the ongoing revolution. His two major works are focused on this task.

Tocqueville's originality as a social and political theorist should not be overlooked. His effort to combine religion and liberty, his proposed remedies to ensure freedom in the midst of equality, his stress on civic engagement, and his understanding of liberty as the active use of essential rights make him stand apart from many other social and political theorists of his time. Tocqueville also excelled at presenting new insights. His exploration of the psychological consequences of democracy, especially in the 1840 portion of his work, with its portrait of *democratic man*, remains fresh and perceptive. And his arguments in *The Old Regime* about the danger of rising expectations, the risk of initial reforms, and the true source of centralization in France were distinctly new and unexpected.

Always the moralist, Tocqueville assumed human responsibility for the outcome of the democratic revolution. The conclusions of the 1835 *Democracy*, Tocqueville declared in a letter, tended toward "the progressive organization of democracy. I have sought... to uncover the natural tendencies a democratic social state gives to human thought and institutions. I have highlighted the dangers awaiting humanity on the way to democracy. But I have not suggested that one cannot fight against these dangers and combat them if diagnosed in time."[5] Would human beings succeed, however, in taming equality and preserving liberty? From 1835 to 1856, Tocqueville grew increasingly pessimistic, even bitter at times. Yet he never completely fell into despair. In drafts for *The Old Regime*, he declared: "I am not, thank God, among those who think that the disease we suffer from is incurable. With a nation so full of contrasts, of reversals, and of resources as ours, I hold that one must never expect too much or fear too much from the future."[6]

In a letter to his friend Eugène Stoffels in 1836, partially cited earlier, Tocqueville attempted to clarify his views. "You believe that

I am going to promote radical and almost revolutionary theories. In that you are wrong. I have shown and will continue to show a keen and reasoned taste for liberty .... I will therefore frankly show this taste for liberty and this general desire to see it develop in all the political institutions of my country; but at the same time, I will profess such a great respect for justice, such a true feeling of love for order and laws, such a profound and reasoned attachment to morality and religious beliefs, that I cannot believe that you will not clearly perceive in me a liberal of a new kind." This letter sounds many of his major and enduring themes: liberty, free institutions, justice, order, moderation, morality, and religion. "There," Tocqueville proclaimed in conclusion, "is my entire plan."[7] He was truly a liberal of a new kind.

Suggestions for Further Reading

The following list, necessarily brief, is intended to guide readers to some of the most essential Tocqueville materials for further reading. Many other valuable titles could be suggested, but readers can use the bibliographies and notes from the following books to find additional items of interest. What is recommended here will point the way to other useful studies and collections. The list, with one exception, includes only English-language volumes. No articles or collections of scholarly essays are included.

The most detailed and informative biography to date is probably the first by André Jardin, *Tocqueville: A Biography*, trans. Lydia Davis (New York: Farrar, Straus and Giroux, 1988), first published in French as *Alexis de Tocqueville (1805–1859)* (Paris: Hachette, 1984).

For English translations of Tocqueville's major works, I recommend: *Democracy in America*, ed. Eduardo Nolla, trans. James T. Schleifer, 2 vols. (Indianapolis: Liberty Fund, 2010), also published as a bilingual French–English edition in 4 volumes; *The Old Regime and the Revolution*, ed. François Furet and Françoise Mélonio, trans. Alan Kahan, 2 vols. (Chicago: University of Chicago Press, 1998/2001); and *Recollections: The French Revolution of 1848 and Its Aftermath*, ed. Olivier Zunz, trans. Arthur Goldhammer (Charlottesville: University of Virginia Press, 2016). All three of these suggestions contain extensive analysis, notes, excerpts from Tocqueville's correspondence, bibliographies, and other important related materials.

On Tocqueville's journey to America, see the classic work by George W. Pierson, *Tocqueville and Beaumont in America* (New York: Oxford University Press, 1938); and the shorter study by Leo Damrosch,

Tocqueville's Discovery of America (New York: Farrar, Straus and Giroux, 2010). For his American travel notes and other pertinent materials, consult *Journey to America*, ed. J. P. Mayer, trans. George Lawrence (New Haven, CT: Yale University Press, 1960); and Olivier Zunz, ed., *Alexis de Tocqueville and Gustave de Beaumont in America: Their Friendship and Their Travels*, trans. Arthur Goldhammer (Charlottesville: University of Virginia Press, 2010).

For Tocqueville and England, the essential work remains Seymour Drescher, *Tocqueville and England* (Cambridge, MA: Harvard University Press, 1964). And for the English and Irish travel diaries, see J. P. Mayer, ed., *Alexis de Tocqueville: Journeys to England and Ireland*, trans. George Lawrence (Garden City, NY: Anchor Books, 1968).

For Tocqueville and France, consult Françoise Mélonio, *Tocqueville and the French*, trans. Beth G. Raps (Charlottesville: University Press of Virginia, 1998), first published as *Tocqueville et les Français* (Paris: Aubier, 1993).

On the themes and development of *Democracy in America*, I suggest my own two studies: *The Chicago Companion to Tocqueville's "Democracy in America"* (Chicago: Chicago University Press, 2012); and *The Making of Tocqueville's "Democracy in America"* (2nd edn., Indianapolis: Liberty Fund, 2000; 1st edn., Chapel Hill: University of North Carolina Press, 1980).

On the writing of *The Old Regime and the Revolution*, readers should consult Robert T. Gannett, *Tocqueville Unveiled: The Historian and His Sources for "The Old Regime and the Revolution"* (Chicago: University of Chicago Press, 2003); and Richard Herr, *Tocqueville and the Old Regime* (Princeton: Princeton University Press, 1962).

For invaluable selections in English from Tocqueville's correspondence, see Roger Boesche, ed., *Alexis de Tocqueville: Selected Letters on Politics and Society*, trans. James Toupin and Roger Boesche (Berkeley: University of California Press, 1985); and Olivier Zunz and Alan S. Kahan, eds., *The Tocqueville Reader: A Life in Letters and Politics* (Oxford: Blackwell Publishing, 2002). For essential selections in French, consult Françoise Mélonio and Laurence Guellec, eds., *Tocqueville: Lettres choisies/Souvenirs 1814–1859* (Paris: Gallimard, 2003).

Concerning Tocqueville's sources and intellectual context, see Aurelian Craiutu, *Liberalism under Siege: The Political Thought of the French Doctrinaires* (Lanham, MD: Lexington Books, 2003); and Jeremy Jennings, *Revolution and the Republic: A History of Political Thought in France Since the Eighteenth Century* (Oxford: Oxford University Press, 2011).

On Tocqueville's ideas concerning the economy and social reform, the key works are Seymour Drescher, ed., *Tocqueville and Beaumont on Social Reform* (New York: Harper and Row, 1968); Michael Drolet, *Tocqueville, Democracy and Social Reform* (New York: Palgrave, 2003); and Richard Swedberg, *Tocqueville's Political Economy* (Princeton: Princeton University Press, 2009).

On Tocqueville and imperialism, consult Jennifer Pitts, ed., *Alexis de Tocqueville: Writings on Empire and Slavery* (Baltimore, MD: Johns Hopkins University Press, 2001).

On Tocqueville and religion, see Alan S. Kahan, *Tocqueville, Democracy, and Religion: Checks and Balances for Democratic Souls* (Oxford: Oxford University Press, 2015).

Notes

Introduction: Tocqueville's Basic Message and His Intellectual Journey

1. Alexis de Tocqueville, *Democracy in America*, ed. Eduardo Nolla, trans. James T. Schleifer, 2 vols., English only edition (Indianapolis: Liberty Fund, 2010), 1: 16, hereafter cited as *DA* (LF). There is also a four-volume French–English bilingual edition; pagination remains the same for both the two-volume and the four-volume editions.

Chapter 1 Alexis de Tocqueville: A Brief Biography

1. See André Jardin, *Tocqueville: A Biography*, trans. Lydia Davis (New York: Farrar, Straus and Giroux, 1988), hereafter cited as Jardin; Hugh Brogan, *Alexis de Tocqueville: A Life* (New Haven: Yale University Press, 2007), hereafter cited as Brogan; and Jean-Louis Benoît, *Tocqueville: Un Destin paradoxal* (Paris: Bayard, 2005). Also see the useful chronologies in Françoise Mélonio and Laurence Guellec, eds., *Tocqueville: Lettres Choisies/Souvenirs 1814–1859* (Paris: Gallimard, 2003), 37–96, hereafter cited as Mélonio, *Lettres*; and Alexis de Tocqueville, *Democracy in America*, ed. Olivier Zunz, trans. Arthur Goldhammer (New York: Library of America, 2004), 878–906, hereafter cited as *DA* (Library of America).
2. Jardin, 82
3. Jardin, 81, letter to Beaumont, October 25, 1829.
4. Jardin, 90, letters to Charles Stoffels, August 26 and October 4, 1830; in Mélonio, *Lettres*, this second letter is dated November 4, 1830.
5. Details of their American journey can be found in several books. See esp. the classic study by George Wilson Pierson, *Tocqueville and*

Beaumont in America (New York: Oxford University Press, 1938) and the shorter work by Leo Damrosch, *Tocqueville's Discovery of America* (New York: Farrar, Straus and Giroux, 2010); also see the discussion in James T. Schleifer, *The Chicago Companion to Tocqueville's "Democracy in America"* (Chicago: University of Chicago Press, 2012), 15-27, hereafter cited as Schleifer, *Chicago Companion*.

6. See Seymour Drescher, *Tocqueville and England* (Cambridge, MA: Harvard University Press, 1964), hereafter cited as Drescher, *England*; and J. P. Mayer, ed., *Alexis de Tocqueville: Journeys to England and Ireland* (Garden City, NY: Anchor Books, 1968); hereafter cited as Mayer, *Journeys to England*.

7. A full catalogue of the works used by Tocqueville may be found in *DA* (LF), 2: 1377–1395.

8. See James T. Schleifer, *The Making of Tocqueville's "Democracy in America,"* 2nd edn. (Indianapolis: Liberty Fund, 2000), 31, hereafter cited as Schleifer, *Making*.

9. Seymour Drescher, ed., *Tocqueville and Beaumont on Social Reform* (New York: Harper and Row, 1968), 1–27, hereafter cited as Drescher, *Social Reform*.

10. See Jennifer Pitts, ed., *Alexis de Tocqueville: Writings on Empire and Slavery* (Baltimore, MD: Johns Hopkins University Press, 2001), 5–26, hereafter cited as Pitts, *Empire and Slavery*. Tocqueville would visit Algeria in 1841 and 1846; consult his additional writings in Pitts, *Empire and Slavery*, 36–58 (travel notes), 59–116 (1841 essay), and 129–98 (1847 reports).

11. See Tocqueville's 1842 report and 1844 speech in Drescher, *Social Reform*, 70–97.

12. See Drescher, *Social Reform*, 98–136; and note Tocqueville's 1843 articles on the topic on pp. 137–173.

13. Roger Boesche, ed. and trans., with James Toupin, trans., *Alexis de Tocqueville: Selected Letters on Politics and Society* (Berkeley: University of California Press, 1985), 146, letter to Royer-Collard, August 15, 1840, hereafter cited as Boesche, *Letters*.

14. Boesche, *Letters*, 155–156, letter to Royer-Collard, September 27, 1841.

15. Boesche, *Letters*, 212, letter to Lord Radnor, May 26, 1848.

16. See Jardin, 346–347 and 350–352, and Drescher, *Social Reform*, 193–200.

17. See Jardin, 388–397; also see Roger Boesche, *Tocqueville's Road Map* (Lanham, MD: Lexington Books, 2006), 189–209, hereafter cited as Boesche, *Road Map*.

18. See Jardin, 398–403.

19. See Françoise Mélonio, ed., *Mélanges, Oeuvres complètes*, vol. XVI (Paris: Gallimard, 1989), 185–198 and 251–269, hereafter cited as *Mélanges*.

20. Quoted in Drescher, *England*, 1, letter to Ampère dated August 1856.

21. Boesche, *Letters*, 377–378, letter to Beaumont, March 4, 1859.
22. Boesche, *Letters*, 156, letter to Royer-Collard, September 27, 1841.
23. See Mélonio, *Lettres*, 814–816; from Tocqueville's *Souvenirs* (*Recollections*).
24. Boesche, *Letters*, 147, letter to Edouard, November 2, 1840; dated September 2, 1840, in Mélonio, *Lettres*, 464.
25. Boesche, *Letters*, 325–326, letter to Madame Swetchine, January 7, 1856.
26. Boesche, *Letters*, 63–64, letter to Charles Stoffels, October 22, 1831.
27. See Jardin, 473–474.
28. Boesche, *Letters*, 93–94, letter to Louis de Kergorlay, January 1835.
29. Boesche, *Letters*, 347–348, letter dated January 24, 1857. Compare this language to Tocqueville's portrait of the new democratic despotism in the 1840 *Democracy*, *DA* (LF), 2: 1249–1252.
30. Schleifer, *Making*, 53–54.
31. Olivier Zunz, ed., *Alexis de Tocqueville and Gustave de Beaumont in America*, trans. Arthur Goldhammer (Charlottesville: University of Virginia Press, 2010), 30, hereafter cited as Zunz, *America*; letter to Hervé de Tocqueville, June 3, 1831.
32. See Aurelian Craiutu and Jeremy Jennings, eds., *Tocqueville on America after 1840* (Cambridge: Cambridge University Press, 2009), and Zunz, *America*, pt. 7.
33. Combining literary or historical writing with a life of politics was not uncommon in early nineteenth-century France; witness Chateaubriand, Lamartine, and Guizot, among many others.
34. See the bibliography compiled by Eduardo Nolla, *DA* (LF), 2: 1377–1395. To have a sense of Tocqueville's printed sources for *The Old Regime*, consult Alexis de Tocqueville, *The Old Regime and the Revolution*, ed. François Furet and Françoise Mélonio, trans. Alan Kahan, 2 vols. (Chicago: University of Chicago Press, 1998), 1: 263–496 and 2: 317–434, hereafter cited as *OR* (Chicago).
35. Consult esp. Robert T. Gannett, *Tocqueville Unveiled: The Historian and His Sources for "The Old Regime and the Revolution"* (Chicago: University of Chicago Press, 2003); Schleifer, *Making*, 103–104, 140–142, 340–342; and editorial notes throughout *DA* (LF). Also see Aurelian Craiutu, *Liberalism Under Siege: The Political Thought of the French Doctrinaires* (Lanham, MD: Lexington Books, 2003), hereafter cited as Craiutu, *Doctrinaires*.
36. Boesche, *Letters*, 130–131, letter to Beaumont, April 22, 1838.
37. See Boesche, *Letters*, 109–110, letter to Royer-Collard, August 25, 1836; and Mélonio, *Lettres*, 358–359, letter to Kergorlay, August 5, 1836.
38. Concerning Montesquieu and Tocqueville, see the classic article by Melvin Richter, "Comparative Political Analysis in Montesquieu and Tocqueville," *Comparative Politics* 1 (1969), 129–160.
39. *DA* (LF), 1: 410.

40. On this period of French political thought, see esp. Jeremy Jennings, *Revolution and the Republic: A History of Political Thought in France Since the Eighteenth Century* (Oxford: Oxford University Press, 2011); and Aurelian Craiutu, *A Virtue for Courageous Minds: Moderation in French Political Thought, 1748–1830* (Princeton: Princeton University Press, 2012).
41. For the essential themes of the *doctrinaires*, consult Craiutu, *Doctrinaires*.
42. See, for example, Boesche, *Letters*, 126–131, letter to Beaumont, April 22, 1838.

Chapter 2 First Principles

1. *DA* (LF), 1: 4–6.
2. *DA* (LF), 1: 6–10.
3. *DA* (LF), 2: 1373.
4. *OR* (Chicago), 1: 259.
5. *DA* (LF), 1: 74 and 74c; also see 1: 75–76, where the definition becomes even more obscure.
6. See Schleifer, *Making*, 13–15.
7. Alexis de Tocqueville, *Recollections, The French Revolution of 1848 and Its Aftermath*, ed. Olivier Zunz, trans. Arthur Goldhammer (Charlottesville: University of Virginia Press, 2016) 45; hereafter cited as *Recollections* (UVA).
8. See, for example, in Tocqueville's travel diaries, *Journey to America*, ed. J. P. Mayer, trans. George Lawrence (New Haven, CT: Yale University Press, 1960), Alphabetic Notebook 1, 181; hereafter cited as Mayer, *Journey to America*.
9. See Schleifer, *Making*, chs. 3–4.
10. *DA* (LF), ch. 1, 1: 33–44, and ch. 2, 1: 45–73.
11. *DA* (LF), 1: 466–467, my emphasis.
12. *DA* (LF), 1: 495 and 499.
13. Boesche, *Letters*, 294, letter to Corcelle, September 17, 1853.
14. *OR* (Chicago), 2: 62.
15. See *DA* (LF), 1: 494–504, and esp. "Importance of What Precedes in Relation to Europe," 1: 505–514.
16. See Schleifer, *Making*, 79–81.
17. *OR* (Chicago), 1: 196–201.
18. *OR* (Chicago), 1: 149 and 235.
19. See Schleifer, *Making*, 215.
20. *DA* (LF), 2: 691–693; also see 2: 986a.
21. *DA* (LF), 2: 1072–1073c. Georges Cuvier (1769–1832) was a great French naturalist.
22. See *DA* (LF), 2: 1054–1057, and *OR* (Chicago) 1: 153.

23. *OR* (Chicago), 1: 153–154.
24. *OR* (Chicago), 1: 321.
25. *DA* (LF), 2: 841v, letter dated November 19, 1831. Cf. Mayer, *Journeys to England*, 53, travel notes dated September 7, 1833.
26. Mélonio, *Lettres*, 410–411, letter dated April 6, 1838, my translation.
27. *DA* (LF), 2: 1281e, Tocqueville's emphasis.
28. *DA* (LF), 2: 853–859, esp. 857–859. Cf. *Recollections* (UVA), 45.
29. Consult Schleifer, *Making*, 82–96.
30. See *DA* (LF), 1: Part II, ch. 10, esp. 515–521 and 548–582.
31. Boesche, *Letters*, 297–301, esp. 299–300, letter dated November 17, 1853; also see 342–348, letter dated January 24, 1857.
32. *DA* (LF), 2: 1284–1285k
33. *DA* (LF), 2: 1284–1285; also see *OR* (Chicago), 2: 377.
34. *DA* (LF), 1: 390; also see 2: 1136.
35. Drescher, *England*, 172, note 6; "Address to the Citizens of Valognes," March 19, 1848.
36. Drescher, *Social Reform*, 181–182, 184, 186–187, speech on the Right to Work, September 1848.
37. *DA* (LF), 2: 1374.
38. *DA* (LF), 1: 26.
39. *OR* (Chicago), 1: 213–216 and 230–231.
40. *Recollections* (UVA), 54–55.
41. *DA* (LF), 1: 32.
42. Boesche, *Letters*, 115–116, letter dated March 22, 1837; also see letter to Kergorlay, December 15, 1850, in Boesche, *Letters*, 257.
43. *OR* (Chicago), 1: 318; also see 2: 27–28.

Chapter 3 Major Themes: Equality, Democracy, Liberty, and Revolution

1. *DA* (LF), 1: 4–6.
2. Boesche, *Letters*, 53–56, letter dated June 29, 1831.
3. *DA* (LF), 2: 1033 note 1.
4. *DA* (LF), 1: 74–90.
5. See the 1840 chapter on servant and master, *DA* (LF), 2: 1013–1015.
6. See, for example, *DA* (LF), 1: 85d and e; and esp. the chapter on the future of the three races in the United States, in *DA* (LF), 1: 515–648.
7. *DA* (LF), 1: 89–90.
8. *DA* (LF), 2: 692e; draft dated June 22, 1838.
9. *OR* (Chicago), 1: 244–246; also see 1: 106, and Tocqueville's notes, 1: 259 and 351.
10. *DA* (LF), 2: 733 and 733h.
11. *DA* (LF), 1: 469.
12. Boesche, *Letters*, 343–344, letter dated January 24, 1857.

13. Mélonio, *Lettres*, 516–518, letter dated September 5, 1843, Tocqueville's emphasis, my translation.
14. *DA* (LF), 1: 89–90.
15. *DA* (LF), 2: 872–80 and 878; also see 872a and b.
16. *OR* (Chicago), 1: 244–246; also see 1: 85–86; 2: 68–69, 151 and 450.
17. For these drafts, see *DA* (LF), 1: 76f, 75–76, my emphasis, and 76g, respectively; also consult Schleifer, *Making*, ch. 19, 325–339.
18. *DA* (LF), 1: 85e; also see the text, 1: 85.
19. *DA* (LF), 2: 780; also see 2: 763b, 771–774 and 772h; also consult in the 1835 *Democracy* the section entitled "Activity That Reigns," in *DA* (LF), 1: 395–401.
20. Olivier Zunz and Alan S. Kahan, eds., *The Tocqueville Reader: A Life in Letters and Politics* (Oxford: Blackwell Publishing, 2002), 250, hereafter cited as Zunz, *Reader*.
21. *OR* (Chicago), 2: 162–163, Tocqueville's emphasis.
22. Mélonio, *Lettres*, 318–319, letter dated April 12, 1835, my translation.
23. *DA* (LF), 2: 1285m.
24. See Drescher, *England*, 121–124; also see Tocqueville's English and Irish travel diaries: Mayer, *Journeys to England*, 42–45, 51–59 and 149–152.
25. *DA* (LF), 1: 400–401; also see the 1840 *Democracy*, in *DA* (LF), 2: 1279–1285.
26. Boesche, *Letters*, 100–102, letter dated June 1835.
27. Boesche, *Letters*, 98–99, letter dated February 21, 1835.
28. *DA* (LF), 2: 1282.
29. *DA* (LF), 2: 1079m.
30. Zunz, *Reader*, 219–220, Tocqueville's emphasis.
31. Zunz, *Reader*, 272, letter dated January 7, 1856.
32. Mayer, *Journeys to England*, 106, remarks written in Dublin, July 7, 1835, Tocqueville's emphasis; Zunz, *Reader*, 219–220; remarks dated 1841.
33. *OR* (Chicago), 1: 216–217; also see 1: 396–397.
34. *DA* (LF), 2: 1262–1277; also see the chapter, "Of the Idea of Rights in the United States," from the 1835 *Democracy*, in *DA* (LF), 1: 389–393.
35. *Mélanges*, 203–220, esp. 206–208. Also see his mention of two other kinds of liberty: "aristocratic" and "bourgeois and democratic," in *DA* (LF), 1: 51.
36. *OR* (Chicago), 1: 249–256.
37. *DA* (LF), 1: 85–86.
38. Boesche, *Letters*, 112–115, letter dated October 5, 1836. To some degree, these comments reflect Guizot's concept of *capacity*. Also see *DA* (LF), 1: 511–513.
39. Boesche, *Letters*, 100–102, letter dated June 1835.
40. Boesche, *Letters*, 355–357, letter dated August 4, 1857.
41. See, for example, *DA* (LF), 2: 876–877; *OR* (Chicago), 1: 216–217.

42. Zunz, *Reader*, 265, letter dated May 13, 1852.
43. *OR* (Chicago), 1: 88; cf. *DA* (LF), 1: 157.
44. *DA* (LF), 1: 68–69.
45. *DA* (LF), 1: 69, Tocqueville's emphasis.
46. *DA* (LF), 1: 16.
47. Zunz, *Reader*, 152–153, letter dated July 24, 1836, my emphasis. Cf. *DA* (LF), 1: 24–26; also see Boesche, *Letters*, 354–355, Tocqueville's letter to Francisque de Corcelle, dated July 29, 1857.
48. Boesche, *Letters*, 365–369, letter dated February 27, 1858.
49. *DA* (LF), 1: 313; also see 1: 455–456.
50. *DA* (LF), 2: 886 and 886c; also see 2: 1273–1274.
51. *DA* (LF), 1: 28o.
52. *Recollections* (UVA), 47–48; also see *OR* (Chicago) 2: 260.
53. *Recollections* (UVA), 4.
54. *DA* (LF), 1: 23f.
55. *DA* (LF), 1: 24; also see 1: 22–26 and 389–390t.
56. See *DA* (LF),1: 628–629z.
57. *DA* (LF), 2: 1273–1274.
58. *DA* (LF), 2: 1273u.
59. *OR* (Chicago), 1: 323–324.
60. *OR* (Chicago), 2: 263–365; also see Boesche, *Letters*, 372–373, letter to Kergorlay, dated May 16, 1858.
61. *DA* (LF), 2: 1133b, Tocqueville's emphasis.
62. See *DA* (LF), 2: 1133–1152 and 780; also consult Drescher, *Social Reform*, 193–200, letters by Tocqueville in *Le Siècle*, January 1843.
63. See *DA* (LF), 2: 951–952 and 1201–1203; *OR* (Chicago), 1: 85–86 and 244–246.
64. On the Glorious Revolution, see *Mélanges*, 558–561, "Quelques notes sur la Révolution de 1688 et 1830," dated 1842.

Chapter 4 Consequences of Democracy: How Does Democracy Change Society?

1. *DA* (LF), 2: 1279b.
2. *DA* (LF), 2: 1279b.
3. See, for example, *DA* (LF), 2: 930–934 and 935–938.
4. *DA* (LF), 2: 931.
5. *DA* (LF), 2: 934g, Tocqueville's emphasis.
6. Mayer, *Journeys to England*, 104–105, from the 1835 travel diaries, July 7, 1835.
7. See Tocqueville's American travel diaries, Mayer, *Journey to America*, 69, 234, 245, 260; Boesche, *Letters*, 39, letter to Ernest de Chabrol, dated June 9, 1831; *DA* (LF), 1: 463–464; and, for England, Mayer, *Journeys to England*, 104–105.

8. See, for example, *DA* (LF), 2: 935–938, esp. 935a, 948–953, and 954–962; about the English middle classes, see *DA* (LF), 960j.
9. *OR* (Chicago), 1: 376; also see 2: 67.
10. *DA* (LF), 2: 951–952; also see 1201–1203.
11. *OR* (Chicago), 1: 85–88; also see 244–246.
12. *DA* (LF), 2: 933–934.
13. *DA* (LF), 2: 767f.
14. *DA* (LF), 2: 1278a. On this matter, Tocqueville completely disagreed with Guizot, who found the middle class the class most capable of governing.
15. *OR* (Chicago), 2: 296–297, from research notes for the incomplete work.
16. See *Recollections* (UVA), 4–5 for these citations; and consult Boesche, *Letters*, 150–151, letter to John Stuart Mill, March 18, 1841.
17. Boesche, *Letters*, 188–189, letter dated August 25, 1847.
18. *DA* (LF), 2: 960–961j, Tocqueville's emphasis.
19. Mayer, *Journeys to England*, 105–106, Dublin, July 7, 1835; also see *DA* (LF) 2: 948–953, esp. 948–950c.
20. See *DA* (LF), 2: 948–953, and 969–979, including notes.
21. *DA* (LF), 2: 788–795 and 813–814.
22. *DA* (LF), 2: 951–952 and 1136–840.
23. *DA* (LF), 2: 881a; consult the chapters on individualism in 2: 881–894.
24. *OR* (Chicago), 1: 178; also 1: 357 and esp. 1: 377. Cf. *DA* (LF), 2: 881–884.
25. *OR* (Chicago), 1: 162–163.
26. *DA* (LF), 2: 980–985.
27. *Recollections* (UVA), 53.
28. Boesche, *Letters*, 354–355, letter dated July 20, 1857.
29. *OR* (Chicago), 1: 170–171; also see 1: 152–163 and 163–171.
30. See *OR* (Chicago),1: 190–192.
31. *OR* (Chicago),1: 87–89.
32. See Schleifer, *Making*, 318, Tocqueville's emphasis.
33. Zunz, *Reader*, 158, letter dated February 3, 1840, Tocqueville's emphasis.
34. *DA* (LF), 1: 407; also see 402–426 (esp. 410–15) and 427–450.
35. *DA* (LF), 1: 412–413; also see 410–415.
36. *DA* (LF), 1: 403 and 249–250, respectively.
37. See *DA* (LF), 1: 410–411, 415, 425 (Tocqueville's own note 6), 427–450, and 630.
38. *DA* (LF), 1: 414 and Tocqueville's own note 4.
39. *DA* (LF), 1: 417 and 419; also see 1: 416–420.
40. *DA* (LF), 2: 718–719 and 724; also consult 711–725.
41. Letter to George C. Lewis, dated October 6, 1856; cited in *OR* (Chicago) 2: 5, Introduction by the editors, my emphasis. Lewis, author and political figure in England, was then Chancellor of the Exchequer.

42. *OR* (Chicago), see esp. 1: 197–198 and 195–202, 202–209, and 209–217.
43. *DA* (LF), 1: 514, Tocqueville's emphasis; also see 1: 505–514, esp. 510–511.
44. See *DA* (LF), 2: 1160–1162 and 1160h; also see 1: 453; *OR* (Chicago), 2: 27 and 185–189.
45. *DA* (LF), 2: 1254o.
46. *Recollections* (UVA), 106.
47. *OR* (Chicago), 2: 247–248.
48. *OR* (Chicago), 2: 185; Boesche, *Letters*, 158, letter to Paul Clamorgam, April 17, 1842; *Mélanges*, 264, my translation; and consult 251–269, esp. 258 and 263–265.
49. Cited in Jardin, 461; also in Mélonio, *Lettres*, 741–743, letter to Jean-Bernardin Rouxel, December 14, 1851.
50. See *DA* (LF), 1: 142–148, esp. 146 and 147, 162–163, and 249–250.
51. See, for example, *DA* (LF), 1: 155–156 and 160–161. Note that he would say the same about the benefits of English decentralization.
52. *DA* (LF), 1: 163.
53. *DA* (LF), 1: 162; also see 1: 148–149 and 249–250.
54. Mayer, *Journeys to England*, 45–46, August 24, 1833, and 62–63, May 11, 1835, Tocqueville's emphasis. Also see the conversation with John Stuart Mill, 66–67, May 26, 1835.
55. *DA* (LF), 1: 505–514, esp. 511.
56. Mélonio, *Lettres*, 418–420; letter dated July 8, 1838, Tocqueville's emphasis, my translation.
57. *DA* (LF), 2: 1249e and 1246; also see 1245–1248, esp. 1247d.
58. See *DA* (LF), 2: 1194–1199, 1200–1205, 1206–1220, 1221–1244, and 1245–1261.
59. *DA* (LF), 2: 1249e, my emphasis.
60. *DA* (LF), 2: 1248–1249.
61. *DA* (LF), 2: 1249–1252; also see the draft dated March 7, 1838, 2: 1247d. Cf. from the 1835 *Democracy*, in *DA* (LF), 1: 157, and from *OR* (Chicago), 1: 377.
62. *OR* (Chicago), 1: 137; cf. 1: 237
63. *OR* (Chicago), 1: 131; also see 1: 118 and 350, 2: 296.
64. *OR* (Chicago), 1: 212.
65. *OR* (Chicago), 1: 213 and 214; cf. *Recollections* (UVA), 53–55, 71–72, 74, 85–86, 96–97, and 118–119.
66. *DA* (LF), 1: 375–401.
67. See *DA* (LF), 1: 395–396.
68. *DA* (LF), 1: 398–399; also see *OR* (Chicago), 2: 304.
69. *DA* (LF), 1: 379; also see *DA* (LF), 1: 383 and 395
70. *DA* (LF), 1: 400. Also consult Richard Swedberg, *Tocqueville's Political Economy* (Princeton: Princeton University Press, 2009), 6–37, hereafter cited as Swedberg, *Political Economy*.
71. *DA* (LF), 1: 382–383.

72. *DA* (LF), 1: 380, and 1: 382–383. Also consult Mélonio, *Lettres*, 591–592, letter to Prosper Enfantin, November 10, 1847.
73. *DA* (LF), 2: 1282.
74. See esp. *DA* (LF), 1: 384–389, 389–393, and 393–395.
75. See, for example, *OR* (Chicago), 1: 87–88.
76. *DA* (LF), 1: 389–391.
77. *DA* (LF), 1: 390.
78. *DA* (LF), 1: 391.
79. *DA* (LF), 1: 391 and 393.
80. See, for example, *DA* (LF), 1: 400–401, and 2: 987–988b, 1091–1092, 1280–1281; also see *OR* (Chicago), 1: 87–88.
81. See *DA* (LF) 1: 89, and 2: 1191–1193 and 1277b.
82. See *DA* (LF), 1: 400–401, and 2: 987–994 and 1031–1040.
83. *DA* (LF), 2: 1006, and 2: 1005–1006 and 1281.
84. See *DA* (LF), 2: 837–838 and 1281.
85. *DA* (LF), 2: 1281, and 1: 400–401, and 2: 1091–1092.
86. See *DA* (LF), 2: 1091, for example.
87. *DA* (LF), 1: 399, and 1: 397–401; also see *OR* (Chicago), 2: 304.
88. *DA* (LF), 2: 987–988b.
89. On apathy, see *DA* (LF), 2: 1150–1051, 1150x and 1293–1294, Tocqueville's own note.
90. See *DA* (LF), 2: 711–725.
91. See *DA* (LF), 2: 759–762; also see *OR* (Chicago), 1: 208 and 223; 2: 29.
92. See *DA* (LF), 2: 942–947.
93. See *DA* (LF), 2: 945–946, and 1203.
94. *DA* (LF), 1: 571.
95. *OR* (Chicago), 1: 402, Tocqueville's notes and drafts, my emphasis; also see 1: 224–225.
96. See, for example, *OR* (Chicago), 1: 96–97; *DA* (LF), 1: 478–488.
97. See the appropriate chapters, *DA* (LF), 2: 1031–1040, 1052–1061, 1062–1067, and 1093–1115.
98. See *DA* (LF), 1: 89; and consult Tocqueville's American travel diaries: Mayer, *Journey to America*, 160; comments dated November 6, 1831.
99. See *DA* (LF), 1: 419 and 489.
100. *DA* (LF), 2: 770g and 774; also see 771–774. Also consult *OR* (Chicago), 2: 258–259.
101. *DA* (LF), 2: 1150–1151; also see 1142–1151.

Chapter 5 Proposed Remedies: What Is To Be Done

1. *DA* (LF), 2: 1275.
2. *DA* (LF), 2: 1264.
3. *DA* (LF), 1: 65.

4. *DA* (LF), 1: 99–114, esp. 111–112; and 1: 142–166, esp. 155–157 and 160–166; and 1: 466.
5. *DA* (LF), 1: 162.
6. *DA* (LF), 1: 165–166.
7. *Recollections* (UVA), 121; and see 119–131.
8. *OR* (Chicago), 1: 127; cf. parallel words in *DA* (LF), 1:157. Also see Tocqueville's explicit comparison of the American town, English parish, and old French parish, in drafts, *OR* (Chicago), 1: 345–346.
9. *OR* (Chicago), 1: 146; also see 1: 160–161, 163, and, from Tocqueville's notes, 2: 332–333.
10. *OR* (Chicago), 1: 249–256, esp. 249 and 250.
11. *OR* (Chicago), 1: 242.
12. See *DA* (LF), 1: 302–312; also 1: 160 and 2: 908–909.
13. See *DA* (LF), 2: 895–904, 905–910 and 911–17, esp. 914 and 917.
14. *DA* (LF), 2: 12680, Tocqueville's emphasis.
15. *DA* (LF), 2: 1269.
16. *DA* (LF), 2: 900.
17. *DA* (LF), 2: 914.
18. *OR* (Chicago), 1: 242–243.
19. *OR* (Chicago), 1: 283, Tocqueville's note 26.
20. *DA* (LF), 1: 252.
21. See *DA* (LF), 1: 246–276; and 1: 465–466 and 497.
22. *DA* (LF), 1: 20–21.
23. *DA* (LF), 1: 387.
24. *DA* (LF), 1: 392v; also see his text, 1: 391; cf. Boesche, *Letters*, 112–115, letter to Eugène Stoffels, October 5, 1836.
25. *DA* (LF), 2: 1272; also see Brogan, 435.
26. *OR* (Chicago), 1: 88.
27. *OR* (Chicago), 1: 195, 198 and 199; for the chapter, see 1: 195–201.
28. See *DA* (LF), 1: 313–314 and 387, text and note r; for full discussions of Tocqueville's views on suffrage, see Alan S. Kahan, *Liberalism in Nineteenth-Century Europe: The Political Culture of Limited Suffrage* (Basingstoke: Palgrave Macmillan, 2003), hereafter cited as Kahan, *Suffrage*; and Robert T. Gannett, Jr., "Tocqueville and the Politics of Suffrage," *The Tocqueville Review: Special Bicentennial Issue*, XXVII, 2: 2006, 209–225, hereafter cited as Gannett, *Suffrage*. In the United States at that time, of course, universal suffrage meant adult *white* males.
29. *DA* (LF), 1: 336–337, 337p, and 404. Tocqueville's views had a significant influence on John Stuart Mill.
30. See Drescher, *Social Reform*, 174–178, Tocqueville's draft of a Manifesto (1847); Gannett, *Suffrage*, 216–218; and Kahan, *Suffrage*, 35–37 and 45–46.
31. Cited in Boesche, *Letters*, 259, note 25.
32. See Mélonio, *Lettres*, 688, letter to Francisque de Corcelle, August 1, 1850.

33. *DA* (LF), 1: 289–301 and 302–312; cf. 2: 905–910 and 2: 1149.
34. *DA* (LF), 1: 305.
35. See Jardin, 350–352.
36. Mélonio, *Lettres*, 688; letter to Francisque de Corcelle, August 1, 1850.
37. See *OR* (Chicago), 1: 202–209, esp. 205–206.
38. *Recollections* (UVA), 119–131, Tocqueville's own account; also consult Jardin, 417–420; Brogan, 451–457.
39. *Recollections* (UVA), 120.
40. See Schleifer, *Making*, 294.
41. *DA* (LF), 1: 385–386 and 384–401.
42. *DA* (LF), 2: 918–925, 926–929, 948–953, and 993.
43. See *DA* (LF), 1: 68–70, 467–488, and 479.
44. See *DA* (LF), 1: 476–477.
45. *OR* (Chicago), 1: 97; cf. variant, 1: 322.
46. Boesche, *Letters*, 294–295, letter dated September 17, 1853; also see Mélonio, *Lettres*, 539, another letter to Corcelle, November 15, 1843; also consult Jardin, 362–368.
47. *DA* (LF), 1: 70, 478–488, esp. 480, 484, 487–488.
48. *DA* (LF), 1: 487–488.
49. *DA* (LF), 2: 961–962; cf. Boesche, *Letters*, 132, to Paul Clamorgam, January 1, 1839.
50. *DA* (LF), 2: 746–747; see Zunz, *Reader*, 227–228, Tocqueville's notes on Islam (1840).
51. *OR* (Chicago), 1: 96–97.
52. *OR* (Chicago), 1: 205.
53. *DA* (LF), 1: 25.
54. *DA* (LF), 1: 117d.
55. *DA* (LF), 1: 158–159.
56. Boesche, *Letters*, 338, dated September 10, 1856; also see 356–357, letter to Kergorlay, August 4, 1857.
57. *DA* (LF), 1: 475.
58. *OR* (Chicago), 1: 206; also see 207–209.
59. *DA* (LF), 1: 70.
60. *OR* (Chicago), 2: 262; and see Mélonio, *Lettres*, 461–462, letter to Royer-Collard, August 15, 1840.
61. *DA* (LF), 2: 1159.
62. See Jardin, 316–342; Pitts, *Empire and Slavery*, esp. the Introduction; Duan Demin, "Reconsidering Tocqueville's Imperialism," *Ethical Perspectives* 17/3 (2010), 415–447; and Cheryl B. Welch, "Colonial Violence and the Rhetoric of Evasion: Tocqueville on Algeria," *Political Theory* 31/2 (2003), 235–264. Also see Tocqueville's praise for European imperialism in general; Boesche, *Letters*, 141–142; letter to Henry Reeve, April 12, 1840.
63. See Zunz, *Reader*, 158, letter to Henry Reeve, February 3, 1840.
64. *DA* (LF), 1: 393.

65. *Recollections* (UVA), 47; see Boesche, *Letters*, 112–115, letter to Eugène Stoffels, October 5, 1836.
66. Mélonio, *Lettres*, 455–456, letter to Henry Reeve, November 15, 1839, Tocqueville's emphasis, my translation.
67. *OR* (Chicago), 1: 86.
68. *DA* (LF), 2: 1279b; also see 1: 512k, my emphasis.

Chapter 6 Economic Ideas and Social Reform

1. See Drescher, *Social Reform*, the pioneering work (1968) and his *Dilemmas of Democracy: Tocqueville and Modernization* (Pittsburgh: University of Pittsburgh Press, 1968); also Jean-Louis Benoît, *Tocqueville moraliste* (Paris: Honoré Champion, 2004); Benoît and Eric Keslassy, eds., *Alexis de Tocqueville: Textes économiques, anthologie critique* (Paris: Pocket, 2005), hereafter cited as Benoît, *Textes*; Boesche, *Road Map*, which contains many of Boesche's articles, including three on economic issues and social reform, items 2 (1981), 3 (1988), and 9 (1983); Michael Drolet, *Tocqueville, Democracy and Social Reform* (New York: Palgrave, 2003), hereafter cited as Drolet, *Social Reform*; Eric Keslassy, *Le Libéralisme de Tocqueville à l'épreuve du paupérisme* (Paris: L'Harmattan, 2000); *Mélanges*, Introduction by Mélonio, as well as many of the documents presented (1989); and Swedberg, *Political Economy*. Also consult the biographies already cited by Jardin, Brogan, and Benoît.
2. See the introduction in Drolet, *Social Reform*; and the introduction and epilogue in Swedberg, *Political Economy*.
3. On Say's influence, see Drolet, *Social Reform*, 39–57; Swedberg, *Political Economy*, 81–83. For Tocqueville's notes on Say, consult *Mélanges*, 425–435.
4. On Senior's influence, see Swedberg, *Political Economy*, 87–91.
5. On Villeneuve-Bargemont's influence, see Drolet, *Social Reform*, 95 and 101–111; and Swedberg, *Political Economy*, 83–86.
6. For example, Drolet, *Social Reform*, and Swedberg, *Political Economy*, both discuss the influence of Adam Smith, Thomas Malthus, David Ricardo, and John Stuart Mill, among others.
7. See Schleifer, *Making*, 97–111; Swedberg, *Political Economy*, 6–37.
8. Mayer, *Journey to America*, from Notebook E, "Means of Increasing Public Prosperity," 270–273.
9. See Mayer, *Journeys to England*, for Tocqueville's travel notes; Drescher, *England*.
10. Mayer, *Journeys to England*, "Exterior Appearance of Manchester," July 2, 1835, 94–95.
11. Mayer, *Journeys to England*, "Visit to the Poorhouse and the University," July 9, 1835, 112.
12. See *DA* (LF), 1: 49e, 85–86d and e, and 345–348.

13. *DA* (LF), 1: 333–356; 1: 454, Tocqueville's own note 1; and 1: 642–643.
14. *DA* (LF), 1: 557–561.
15. *DA* (LF), 1: 74–90, esp. 79–80.
16. *DA* (LF), 2: 980–985; cf. 1025–1030.
17. *DA* (LF), 2: 982.
18. *DA* (LF), 2: 771–772.
19. *DA* (LF), 2: 1241.
20. *DA* (LF), 2: 1232 and 1238.
21. *Recollections* (UVA), 45 and 62.
22. *OR* (Chicago), 1: 157; also see 2: 336–337.
23. On the economic achievements of the Revolution, see *OR* (Chicago), 2: 201–204.
24. See Mélonio, *Lettres*, 307–308, letter to Kergorlay, September 28, 1834.
25. For the 1835 essay, see Drescher, *Social Reform*, 1–27.
26. Drescher, *Social Reform*, 24–25.
27. For the 1837 piece, see *Mélanges*, 140–157.
28. See Drescher, *Social Reform*, 98–136. For Tocqueville's 1843 writings on emancipation, see Drescher, *Social Reform*, 137–173; Pitts, *Empire and Slavery*, 199–226.
29. Drescher, *Social Reform*, 102.
30. See Drescher, *Social Reform*, 193–200, esp. 200; and consult Jardin, 350–352.
31. See Boesche, *Road Map*, 189–209; also see Jardin, 386–403; Drolet, *Social Reform*, 153–160.
32. See Drescher, *Social Reform*, 174–178; Benoît, *Textes*, 183–191; also consult Drolet, *Social Reform*, 161–162; Swedberg, *Political Economy*, 169–170.
33. Zunz, *Reader*, 224–225.
34. See Drolet, *Social Reform*, 161–173; also see Benoît, *Textes*, 322–351.
35. See Drescher, *Social Reform*, 179–192, esp. 192.
36. Boesche, *Letters*, 211–212, letter to Lord Radnor, May 26, 1848.
37. For example, see Tocqueville's Introduction to his 1835 book, in *DA* (LF), 1: 16.
38. *DA* (LF), 2: 1371, letter to Charles Stoffels, April 21, 1830.
39. Mayer, *Journeys to England*, 83–86, "Deduction of Ideas," June 25–30, 1835, Tocqueville's emphasis.
40. *DA* (LF), 2: 1030.
41. *DA* (LF), 2: 1232; cf. 2: 1238 and 1265. Tocqueville opens his examination of industrialization (2: 1231–1241) by discussing the growing number of industrial properties and owners of such property (the industrialists) and pointing out how such property is less bound or protected by rules, regulations, and precedent than landed property. In his own note (#5), he mentions the owners of mines and then, in his text, continues by presenting the increasing multitude of indus-

trial associations – corporations – and acknowledging the case for their regulation.

42. *DA* (LF), 2: 1255p.
43. *DA* (LF), 2: 1265.
44. *DA* (LF), 2: 903–904, not finally included.
45. *DA* (LF), 2: 869–870h, not finally included; cf. 2: 775a.
46. Zunz, *Reader*, 250.
47. *OR* (Chicago), 1: 378, from Tocqueville's drafts.
48. Boesche, *Letters*, 96–98, letter to Nassau William Senior, February 21, 1835; the discussion involves the 1835 translation by Henry Reeve; also see *DA* (LF), 1: 382–383, text and note j.
49. Mélonio, *Lettres*, 591–592; letter to Prosper Enfantin, November 10, 1847, my translation.
50. Boesche, *Letters*, 336–337; letter to Sophie Swetchine, September 10, 1856.
51. Mélonio, *Lettres*, 516–518; letter to Gobineau, September 5, 1843, Tocqueville's emphasis, my translation.
52. See *DA* (LF), 1: 517, 526–527, and 554–555.
53. *DA* (LF), 1: 414.
54. *OR* (Chicago), 1: 117–118.
55. See, for example, Drolet, *Social Reform*, 52–53, and elsewhere in Drolet's book.
56. Mayer, *Journeys to England*, 97, note 43, Manchester, July 2, 1835.
57. *DA* (LF), 2: 982.

Chapter 7 Tocqueville's Reputation and Continuing Relevance

1. See Françoise Mélonio, *Tocqueville and the French*, trans. Beth G. Raps (Charlottesville: University Press of Virginia, 1998), 94–97 and 149, hereafter cited as Mélonio, *Tocqueville and the French*; originally published as *Tocqueville et les Français* (Paris: Aubier, 1993).
2. Consult Jardin, 224–230, 500–508 and 517, and Brogan, 283–304, 344–346, 562–565 and 587–596. For Gosselin's remark, see Jardin, 224. Also see Richard Herr, *Tocqueville and the Old Regime* (Princeton: Princeton University Press, 1962), 89–91 and 107–119.
3. *Democracy in America*, ed. and trans. Harvey C. Mansfield and Delba Winthrop (Chicago: University of Chicago Press, 2000); see Mansfield's Introduction, xvii, hereafter cited as *DA* (Chicago).
4. François Furet, *Interpreting the French Revolution*, trans. Elborg Forster (Cambridge: Cambridge University Press, 1981), 16; originally published as *Penser la Révolution Française* (Paris: Gallimard, 1978).
5. On Tocqueville's reception and reputation in the United States, see Matthew Mancini, "Too Many Tocquevilles: The Fable of Tocqueville's

American Reception," *Journal of the History of Ideas* 69/2 (April 2008), 245–268; "From Oblivion to Apotheosis: The Ironic Journey of Alexis de Tocqueville," *Journal of American Studies* 45/1 (Feb. 2011), 21–37; and *Alexis de Tocqueville and American Intellectuals: From His Times to Ours* (Lanham, MD: Rowman and Littlefield, 2006), chs. 4, 5, and 6, hereafter cited as Mancini, *American Intellectuals*. For the contrary view, see Robert Nisbet, "Many Tocquevilles," *The American Scholar* 46 (Winter 1976–77), 59–75. Also consult James T. Kloppenberg, "Life Everlasting: Tocqueville in America," in his *The Virtues of Liberalism* (New York: Oxford University Press, 1998), 71–81; Isaac Kramnick's Introduction in *Democracy in America*, ed. Kramnick, trans. Gerald E. Bevan (London: Penguin Books, 2003), ix–xlviii, hereafter cited as *DA* (Penguin); James T. Schleifer, "*Democracy in America* in the United States," in *Alexis de Tocqueville*, introduction and notes by Jean-Claude Lamberti and Françoise Mélonio (Paris: Laffont, 1986), 667–699; and Olivier Zunz, "Tocqueville and the Americans: *Democracy in America* as Read in Nineteenth-Century America," in Cheryl B. Welch, ed., *The Cambridge Companion to Tocqueville* (Cambridge: Cambridge University Press, 2006), 359–396.

6. The new translations and editions of *Democracy in America* have already been cited: *DA* (Chicago) in 2000; *DA* (Penguin) in England in 2003; *DA* (Library of America) in 2004; and *DA* (LF) in 2010. The new translation and critical edition of *The Old Regime* has also been cited: *OR* (Chicago), 1998/2001. Also see *Recollections* (UVA), 2016.

7. See Mélonio, *Tocqueville and the French*, esp. chs. 4, 5, and 6.

8. Brogan (originally 2006); a short biographical study, *The Prophet of the Mass Age*, was published earlier by J. P. Mayer (London: J. M. Dent and Sons, 1939).

9. See various articles by Reiji Matsumoto, "Tocqueville and Japan," in Aurelian Craiutu and Sheldon Gellar, eds., *Conversations With Tocqueville: The Global Democratic Revolution in the Twenty-first Century* (Lanham, MD: Lexington Books, 2009), 295–317, hereafter cited as Craiutu, *Conversations*; and "Tocqueville and Democracy in Japan," in Christine Dunn Henderson, ed., *Tocqueville's Voyages: The Evolution of His Ideas and Their Journey Beyond His Time* (Indianapolis: Liberty Fund, 2014), 425–455; hereafter cited as Henderson, *Voyages*. Also consult the special issue on China, Japan, and Tocqueville, *The Tocqueville Review* 38/1 (2017), which includes articles by Reiji Matsumoto, Hiroshi Watanabe, and Yasutake Miyashiro.

10. See Jianxun Wang, "The Road to Democracy in China: A Tocquevillian Analysis," in Craiutu, *Converations*, 271–294; Li Hongtu, "Transformation des sociétés et naissance des révolutions: La mode de Tocqueville dans la Chine actuelle," *The Tocqueville Review* 36/1 (2015), 215–233; and the articles by Ming Chong and Cheryl Welch in the special issue of *The Tocqueville Review* 38/1 (2017).

11. See Craiutu, *Conversations*; Henderson, *Voyages*; Ewa Atanassow and Richard Boyd, eds., *Tocqueville and the Frontiers of Democracy* (Cambridge: Cambridge University Press, 2013); and Joshua Mitchell, *Tocqueville in Arabia* (Chicago: University of Chicago Press, 2013).

12. Boesche, *Letters*, 149–152, letter to John Stuart Mill, March 18, 1841.

13. On this topic, see Jill Locke and Eileen Hunt Botting, eds., *Feminist Interpretations of Alexis de Tocqueville* (University Park: Pennsylvania State University Press, 2009).

14. On Mill, in addition to his own writings, see Dale E. Miller, *J. S. Mill* (Cambridge: Polity, 2010); Ross Harrison, "John Stuart Mill, mid-Victorian," in Gareth Stedman Jones and Gregory Claeys, eds., *The Cambridge History of Nineteenth-Century Political Thought* (Cambridge: Cambridge University Press, 2011), 295–318; the classic article by H. O. Pappe, "Mill and Tocqueville," *Journal of the History of Ideas* 25/2 (1964), 217–234; and Swedberg, *Political Economy*, 91–99.

15. On Weber, in addition to *The Protestant Ethic and the Spirit of Capitalism* (1905) and *Economy and Society* (1922) and other works, see the essay by Antonino Palumbo and Alan Scott, "Weber, Durkheim and the Sociology of the Modern State," in Terrence Ball and Richard Bellamy, eds., *The Cambridge History of Twentieth-Century Political Thought* (Cambridge: Cambridge University Press, 2003), 368–391; and Alan Kahan, *Tocqueville, Democracy, and Religion* (Oxford: Oxford University Press, 2015), 195–212.

16. On Arendt, in addition to *The Origins of Totalitarianism* (1951), see Mancini, *American Intellectuals*, 228–236; Boesche, "Tocqueville and Arendt on the Novelty of Modern Tyranny," in *Road Map*, 169–188; and Jeffrey C. Isaac, "Critics of Totalitarianism," in *The Cambridge History of Twentieth-Century Political Thought*, 181–201. My brief discussion largely summarizes Boesche's essay.

17. On Hayek, in addition to *The Road to Serfdom* (1944) and *The Constitution of Liberty* (1960) and other works, see Chandran Kukathas, *Hayek and Modern Liberalism* (Oxford: Clarendon Press, 1989). Also see Benoît, *Textes*, 135–194. A forthcoming book on Tocqueville and Hayek, coauthored by Christine Dunn Henderson and Chadran Kukathas, is scheduled to appear in 2019.

18. See, in addition to Sandel's other works, Michael J. Sandel, *Justice: What's the Right Thing to Do?* (New York: Farrar, Straus and Giroux, 2009); and David Miller and Richard Dagger, "Utilitarianism and Beyond: Contemporary Analytical Political Theory," in *The Cambridge History of Twentieth-Century Political Thought*, 446–469.

19. Thomas Piketty, *Capital in the Twenty-First Century*, trans. Arthur Goldhammer (Cambridge, MA: The Belknap Press, 2014); originally published as *Le Capital au XXI siècle* (Paris: Editions du Seuil, 2013).

20. *DA* (LF), 1: 76–85.

21. Boesche, *Letters*, 98–100, letter to Eugène Stoffels, February 21, 1835.

Conclusion

1. See, for example, Boesche, *Letters*, 191, letter to Kergorlay, October 18, 1847.
2. *DA* (LF), 1: 515–648, esp. 515–582.
3. Consult Mayer, *Journey*, 217–219 and 258–261; also see *DA* (LF), 2: 735m.
4. See, for example, Boesche, *Letters*, 354–355 and 355–357, letters to Corcelle, July 29, 1857, and to Kergorlay, August 4, 1857.
5. Zunz, *Reader*, 136–137, letter to Francisque de Corcelle, April 12, 1835.
6. *OR* (Chicago), 1: 316.
7. Mélonio, *Lettres*, 352–353, letter to Eugène Stoffels, July 24, 1836, my translation.

Works Cited and Consulted

Arendt, Hannah. *The Origins of Totalitarianism*. New York: Harcourt, Brace, 1951.

Atanassow, Ewa and Richard Boyd, eds. *Tocqueville and the Frontiers of Democracy*. Cambridge: Cambridge University Press, 2013.

Ball, Terence and Richard Bellamy, eds. *Cambridge History of Twentieth-Century Political Thought*. Cambridge: Cambridge University Press, 2003.

Benoît, Jean-Louis. *Tocqueville moraliste*. Paris: Honoré Champion, 2004.

Benoît, Jean-Louis. *Tocqueville: Un destin paradoxal*. Paris: Bayard, 2005.

Benoît, Jean-Louis and Eric Keslassy, eds. *Alexis de Tocqueville: Textes économiques, anthologie critique*. Paris: Pocket, 2005.

Boesche, Roger, ed. *Alexis de Tocqueville: Selected Letters on Politics and Society*, trans. James Toupin and Roger Boesche. Berkeley: University of California Press, 1985.

Boesche, Roger. *Tocqueville's Road Map*. Lanham, MD: Lexington Books, 2006.

Brogan, Hugh. *Alexis de Tocqueville: A Life*. New Haven, CT: Yale University Press, 2007.

Craiutu, Aurelian. "Tocqueville and the Political Thought of the French Doctrinaires (Guizot, Royer-Collard, Rémusat)." *History of Political Thought* XX/3 (1999), 456–493.

Craiutu, Aurelian. *Liberalism under Siege: The Political Thought of the French Doctrinaires*. Lanham, MD: Lexington Books, 2003.

Craiutu, Aurelian. *A Virtue for Courageous Minds: Moderation in French Political Thought, 1748–1830*. Princeton: Princeton University Press, 2012.

Craiutu, Aurelian and Sheldon Gellar, eds. *Conversations with Tocqueville: The Global Democratic Revolution in the Twenty-First Century*. Lanham, MD: Lexington Books, 2009.

Craiutu, Aurelian and Jeremy Jennings, eds. *Tocqueville on America after 1840*. Cambridge: Cambridge University Press, 2009.

Damrosch, Leo. *Tocqueville's Discovery of America*. New York: Farrar, Straus and Giroux, 2010.

Drescher, Seymour. *Tocqueville and England*. Cambridge, MA: Harvard University Press, 1964.

Drescher, Seymour. *Dilemmas of Democracy: Tocqueville and Modernization*. Pittsburgh, PA: University of Pittsburgh Press, 1968.

Drescher, Seymour, ed. *Tocqueville and Beaumont on Social Reform*. New York: Harper and Row, 1968.

Drolet, Michael. *Tocqueville, Democracy and Social Reform*. New York: Palgrave, 2003.

Duan, Demin. "Reconsidering Tocqueville's Imperialism." *Ethical Perspectives* 17/3 (2010), 415–447.

Eisenstadt, Abraham S., ed. *Reconsidering Tocqueville's "Democracy in America."* New Brunswick: Rutgers University Press, 1988.

Furet, François. *Interpreting the French Revolution*, trans. Elborg Forster. Cambridge: Cambridge University Press, 1981.

Gannett, Robert T. *Tocqueville Unveiled: The Historian and His Sources for "The Old Regime and the Revolution."* Chicago: University of Chicago Press, 2003.

Gannett, Robert T. "Tocqueville and the Politics of Suffrage." *The Tocqueville Review: Special Bicentennial Issue* XXVII/2 (2006), 209–225.

Guellec, Laurence. *Tocqueville et les langages de la démocratie*. Paris: Honoré Champion, 2004.

Hayek, Friedrich. *The Road to Serfdom*. Chicago, IL: University of Chicago Press, 1944.

Hayek, Friedrich. *The Constitution of Liberty*. Chicago, IL: University of Chicago Press, 1960.

Henderson, Christine Dunn, ed. *Tocqueville's Voyages: The Evolution of His Ideas and Their Journey Beyond His Time*. Indianapolis, IN: Liberty Fund, 2014.

Herr, Richard. *Tocqueville and the Old Regime*. Princeton, NJ: Princeton University Press, 1962.

Jardin, André. *Tocqueville: A Biography*, trans. Lydia Davis. New York: Farrar, Straus and Giroux, 1988. Originally published in French as *Alexis de Tocqueville (1805–1859)*. Paris: Hachette, 1984.

Jaume, Lucien. *Tocqueville: The Aristocratic Sources of Liberty*, trans. Arthur Goldhammer. Princeton, NJ: Princeton University Press, 2013. Originally published as *Tocqueville: Les sources aristocratiques de la liberté*. Paris: Fayard, 2008.

Jennings, Jeremy. *Revolution and the Republic: A History of Political Thought in France since the Eighteenth Century*. Oxford: Oxford University Press, 2011.

Jones, Gareth Stedman and Gregory Claeys, eds. *Cambridge History of Nineteenth-Century Political Thought*. Cambridge: Cambridge University Press, 2011.

Kahan, Alan S. *Aristocratic Liberalism: The Social and Political Thought of Jacob Burckhardt, John Stuart Mill and Alexis de Tocqueville*. New York: Oxford University Press, 1992.

Kahan, Alan S. *Liberalism in Nineteenth-Century Europe: The Political Culture of Limited Suffrage*. Basingstoke: Palgrave Macmillan, 2003.

Kahan, Alan S. *Alexis de Tocqueville*. New York: Continuum, 2010.

Kahan, Alan S. *Tocqueville, Democracy, and Religion: Checks and Balances for Democratic Souls*. Oxford: Oxford University Press, 2015.

Keslassy, Eric. *Le Libéralisme de Tocqueville à l'épreuve du paupérisme*. Paris: L'Harmattan, 2000.

Kloppenberg, James T. *The Virtues of Liberalism*. New York: Oxford University Press, 1998.

Kukathas, Chandran. *Hayek and Modern Liberalism*. Oxford: Clarendon Press, 1989.

Lamberti, Jean-Claude and Françoise Mélonio, eds. In the Bouquin series. *Alexis de Tocqueville*. Paris: Robert Laffont, 1986.

Li Hongtu. "Transformation des sociétés et naissance des révolutions: La mode de Tocqueville dans la Chine actuelle." *The Tocqueville Review* 36/1 (2015), 215–233.

Lively, Jack. *The Social and Political Thought of Alexis de Tocqueville*. Oxford: Clarendon Press, 1965.

Locke, Jill and Eileen Hunt Botting, eds. *Feminist Interpretations of Alexis de Tocqueville*. University Park: Pennsylvania State University Press, 2009.

Mancini, Matthew. *Alexis de Tocqueville and American Intellectuals: From His Times to Ours*. Lanham, MD: Rowman and Littlefield, 2006.

Mancini, Matthew. "Too Many Tocquevilles: The Fable of Tocqueville's American Reception." *Journal of the History of Ideas* 69/2 (April 2008), 245–268.

Mancini, Matthew. "From Oblivion to Apotheosis: The Ironic Journey of Alexis de Tocqueville." *Journal of American Studies* 45/1 (February 2011), 21–37.

Manent, Pierre. *Tocqueville et la nature de la démocratie*. Paris: Julliard, 1982.

Mansfield, Harvey. *Tocqueville: A Very Short Introduction*. Oxford: Oxford University Press, 2010.

Mayer, J. P. *The Prophet of the Mass Age*. London: J. M. Dent and Sons, 1939.

Mélonio, Françoise, ed. *Mélanges*, volume XVI of *Alexis de Tocqueville, Oeuvres complètes*. Paris: Gallimard, 1989.

Mélonio, Françoise. *Tocqueville and the French*, trans. Beth G. Raps. Charlottesville: University Press of Virginia, 1998. Originally published as *Tocqueville et les Français*. Paris: Aubier, 1993.

Mill, John Stuart. *Considerations on Representative Government*. London: Parker, Son, and Bourn, 1861.

Mill, John Stuart. *On Liberty and Other Essays*. New York: Kaplan, 2009.

Miller, Dale E. *J. S. Mill*. Cambridge: Polity, 2010.

Mitchell, Joshua. *The Fragility of Freedom*. Chicago, IL: Chicago University Press, 1995.

Mitchell, Joshua. *Tocqueville in Arabia*. Chicago, IL: University of Chicago Press, 2013.

Nisbet, Robert. "Many Tocquevilles." *The American Scholar* 46 (Winter 1976–77), 59–75.

Nolla, Eduardo, ed. *Liberty, Equality, Democracy*. New York: New York University Press, 1992.

Pappe, H. O. "Mill and Tocqueville." *Journal of the History of Ideas* 25/2 (1964), 217–234.

Pierson, George Wilson. *Tocqueville and Beaumont in America*. New York: Oxford University Press, 1938.

Piketty, Thomas. *Capital in the Twenty-First Century*, trans. Arthur Goldhammer. Cambridge, MA: Belknap Press, 2014. Originally published as *Le Capital au XXI siècle*. Paris: Editions du Seuil, 2013.

Pitts, Jennifer, ed. *Alexis de Tocqueville: Writings on Empire and Slavery*. Baltimore, MD: Johns Hopkins University Press, 2001.

Richter, Melvin. "Comparative Political Analysis in Montesquieu and Tocqueville." *Comparative Politics* 1 (1969), 129–160.

Richter, Melvin. "Tocqueville on Algeria." *Review of Politics* 25/3 (July 1963), 362–398.

Sandel, Michael J. *Democracy's Discontent: America in Search of a Public Philosophy*. Cambridge, MA: Belknap Press, 1996.

Sandel, Michael J. *Justice: What's the Right Thing to Do?* New York: Farrar, Straus and Giroux, 2009.

Schleifer, James T. *The Making of Tocqueville's "Democracy in America."* 2nd edn. Indianapolis, IN: Liberty Fund, 2000; 1st edn. Chapel Hill, NC: University of North Carolina Press, 1980.

Schleifer, James T. *The Chicago Companion to Tocqueville's "Democracy in America."* Chicago, IL: University of Chicago Press, 2012.

Schleifer, James T. "Tocqueville, Religion, and 'Democracy in America': Some Essential Questions." *American Political Thought* 3 (Fall 2014), 254–272.

Siedentop, Larry. *Tocqueville*. Oxford: Oxford University Press, 1994.

Shiner, Larry E. *The Secret Mirror: Literary Form and History in Tocqueville's "Recollections."* Ithaca, NY: Cornell University Press, 1988.

Swedberg, Richard. *Tocqueville's Political Economy*. Princeton, NJ: Princeton University Press, 2009.

Tocqueville. *Journey to America*, ed. J. P. Mayer, trans. George Lawrence. New Haven, CT: Yale University Press, 1960.

Tocqueville. *Journeys to England and Ireland*, ed. J. P. Mayer, trans. George Lawrence. Garden City, NY: Anchor Books, 1968.

Tocqueville. *The Old Regime and the Revolution*, ed. François Furet and Françoise Mélonio, trans. Alan Kahan, 2 vols. Chicago, IL: University of Chicago Press, 1998/2001.

Tocqueville. *Democracy in America*, ed. and trans. Harvey C. Mansfield and Delba Winthrop. Chicago, IL: University of Chicago Press, 2000.

Tocqueville. *Democracy in America*, ed. Isaac Kramnick, trans. Gerald E. Bevan. London: Penguin Books, 2003.

Tocqueville. *Lettres choisies/Souvenirs 1814–1859*, ed. Françoise Mélonio and Laurence Guellec. Paris: Gallimard, 2003.

Tocqueville. *Democracy in America*, ed. Olivier Zunz and Arthur Goldhammer, trans. Arthur Goldhammer. New York: Library of America, 2004.

Tocqueville. *Democracy in America*, ed. Eduardo Nolla, trans. James T. Schleifer. A translation of the 1990 Vrin historical-critical edition, 2 vols. Indianapolis, IN: Liberty Fund, 2010. Also published as a bilingual French–English edition in 4 vols. Because the French–English is done as facing pages, pagination is the same in the two versions.

Tocqueville. *Recollections: The French Revolution of 1848 and Its Aftermath*, ed. Olivier Zunz, trans. Arthur Goldhammer. Charlottesville: University of Virginia Press, 2016.

Tocqueville Review 38/1 (2017). Special issue on Tocqueville, China, and Japan.

Weber, Max. *The Protestant Ethic and the Spirit of Capitalism*, trans. Talcott Parsons. New York: Scribner, 1958.

Weber, Max. *Economy and Society: An Outline of Interpretive Sociology*, ed. Guenther Roth and Claus Wittich, trans. Ephraim Fischoff and others. New York: Bedminster Press, 1968.

Welch, Cheryl B. *De Tocqueville*. New York: Oxford University Press, 2001.

Welch, Cheryl B. "Colonial Violence and the Rhetoric of Evasion: Tocqueville on Algeria." *Political Theory* 31/2 (2003), 235–264.

Welch, Cheryl B., ed. *The Cambridge Companion to Tocqueville*. Cambridge: Cambridge University Press, 2006.

Zuckert, Catherine. "Not by Preaching: Tocqueville on the Role of Religion in American Democracy." *The Review of Politics* 43/2 (April 1981), 259–280.

Zunz, Olivier, ed. Arthur Goldhammer, trans. *Alexis de Tocqueville and Gustave de Beaumont in America: Their Friendship and Their Travels*. Charlottesville: University of Virginia Press, 2010.

Zunz, Olivier and Alan S. Kahan, eds. *The Tocqueville Reader: A Life in Letters and Politics*. Oxford: Blackwell Publishing, 2002.

Index